"Going the Extra Mile": Security through Separation

Echo on a Chip

A New Perception for the Next Generation of Micro-Controllers handling Encryption for Mobile Messaging: From Secure Embedded Systems to Separated Secure Embedded Systems (SSES) in Cryptography

Hardware supported Trusted Execution Environments (TEE) for Encryption / Decryption Processes separated from Transport-Processes and Server-Processes respective even other Operational Processes

Mancy A. Wake
Dorothy Hibernack
Lucas Lullaby

Impressum:

Wake, Mancy A. / Hibernack, Dorothy / Lullaby, Lucas:
   Echo on a Chip (EoC)
   - A New Perception for the Next Generation of Micro-
   Controllers handling Encryption for Mobile Messaging:
   From Secure Embedded Systems to Separated Secure
   Embedded Systems (SSES) in Cryptography.
   Hardware supported Trusted Execution Environments
   (TEE) for Encryption / Decryption Processes separated
   from Transport-Processes and Server-Processes
   respective even other Operational Processes.
   Norderstedt 2020
   ISBN 9783751916448

Manufacturer / Publisher / Printing:
BoD - Books on Demand, Norderstedt - http://www.bod.de
© 2020 Mancy A. Wake / Dorothy Hibernack / Lucas Lullaby
More bibliographic info under: https://portal.dnb.de

9 783751 916448

Echo on a Chip

Echo on a C
Echo on a Chi
Echo on a Chip
Echo on a Chip
Echo on a Chip

**A New Perception for the
Next Generation of Micro-Controllers
handling Multi-Encryption for Mobile Messaging**

From Secure Embedded Systems to
Separated Secure Embedded Systems (SSES)
in Cryptography

Hardware supported
Trusted Execution Environments (TEE)

EoC
#1

Mancy A. Wake
Dorothy Hibernack
Lucas Lullaby

Structure:

ABSTRACT:
Going the Extra Mile - Security through Separation

Based on the historical development of so-called Crypto-Chips, the current transformation of cryptography shows numerous changes, innovations and new process designs in the field of cryptography, which also need to be integrated in a hardware design of microprocessors and micro-controllers for a secure embedded system.

Single-board computers like Raspberry Pi or Arduino and also devices with cryptographic functions such as the NitroKey and others allow developers to create their design architectures accordingly.

Using the example of the encrypting Echo protocol, a design of a hardware architecture based on three chips with cryptographic functions corresponding to the protocol is described.

The central echo chip # 1 represents a "Trusted Execution Environment" (TEE), which is not connected to the Internet for the conversion processes from plaintext to ciphertext and is supposed to remain quasi original, to prevent software injections or possible uploads of copies of the plaintext.

The export and transport of the encrypted Echo capsules can then be regulated using other ways, methods and protocols than TCP. The same applies to deciphering the packets to be delivered.

The two other chips then take over predominantly routing, respective forwarding and further server functions.

The technical specifications of the three microprocessors for the individual functions of Echo and encryption are described in detail.

The established paradigm of separation is recognized as a security feature and discussed as a perception for a next generation of micro-controllers in the field of mobile messaging under the technical term "Going the Extra Mile". Going the Extra Mile means using your own platform or hardware that is separate from the network for the conversion from plaintext to ciphertext and vice versa.

This security architecture is then discussed in the context of seven different current risk cases with the consolidated result that the well-known OSI (Open Systems Interconnection) model can be expanded to a thirteen-stage model: This essay introduces the basis of the Secure Architecture Model, abbreviated SAM, that integrates the previous OSI model and builds on it to examine the further effects and further research needs for a department of cryptography and its related disciplines, in particular the Secure Embedded Systems and as well other areas.

11

1 Historic development of Cryptographic Chips: From Enigma to Ecolex and AroFlex

In the past, cryptographic micro-controllers had primarily these functions since their first development in the mid-1970s (e.g. by Philips Usfa Crypto) - roughly in line with the spread of asymmetric encryption of a public key infrastructure (PKI):

- to carry out the encryption with the aid of a computer with a dedicated computing machine
- to offer the process to dedicated customers such as military or individual governments
- to convert ciphertext faster or more adapted to possibly more complex algorithms of the respective era
- respective to relate it in particular to the encryption of speech
- or to operate different channels in parallel –
- and above all: to include an uninfluenced, hardware-supported number generator.

Previously, the development of the Crypto-Chips was based on symmetrical encryption, just as Philips started with a one-time tape (OTT) called ECOLEX in 1956 (Philips Usfa 1982).

The Crypto-Chips digitized the previously mechanical encryption processes in an electronic processor, e.g. of the Enigma machines that have been developed by Chiffriermaschinen AG since the mid-1920s.

In the architectures, several chips were often chained one after the other in order to map cryptographic routines, for example to implement a stream cipher: Eight such chips were e.g. connected in the AroFlex machine. They were also called "crypto hearts" (Kraan 1986).

Likewise, a lot has been technically adapted over the years to make the chips more contemporary in their hardware, for example in the case of the transistors, or to adapt them to the general chip development. Today, single-board computers such as Raspberry Pi or Arduino and others are available and programmable for everyone.

The security of the uses of these "embedded systems" remains to be assessed and designed according to modern processes and standards of cryptography.

Other crypto machines that also used microprocessors, such as those from Crypto AG, were manipulated.

The Secret Service Coup of the Century first went public in 2020: The CIA and the German BND had bought the Swiss Crypto AG in 1970 under cover behind trustees. The hardware produced had been manipulated in order to be able to intercept governments from more than 100 countries that were customers of Crypto AG (Miller et al. 2020).

Hence, the development of secure embedded systems remains a hot topic for cryptography in the face of these disclosed historical developments.

2 Transformation of Cryptography influences Secure Embedded Systems in a Network

The more recent developments in cryptography in the 21st century are not only one-sided towards future quantum cryptography (PQCrypto 2019, Zimmermann 2019), but are already showing today fundamental changes in numerous existing processes:

It starts with multi-encryption, goes via Instant Perfect Forward Secrecy (IPFS) with end-to-end encryption with Cryptographic Calling, the adaptation of cryptographic protocols as through Fiasco Forwarding, in which up to a dozen keys out of a pool are used to decode a message.

It continues to solve the key transport problem with Secret Streams and Juggerknaut keys to a volatile and Exponential Encryption.

In their book "Transformation of Cryptography", the authors Linda Bertram and Gunther van Dooble (2019) have, for example, compiled over two dozen of these changes and innovative concepts that are currently influencing cryptography and whose transformation characterizes them: One can currently speak of a "Transformation of Cryptography".

The transformation is therefore not just about the step into cryptography that is resistant to the fast computing operations of quantum computers, for example by exchanging the RSA algorithm with algorithms such as NTRU or McEliece (ibid 1978), but also about numerous development steps, which are emerging in multiple, also process-oriented ways, such as multi-encryption and new Internet protocols such as the Echo protocol (Gasakis / Schmidt 2018), which combines multi-encryption with aspects of graph theory.

Why shouldn't the newer cryptographic innovations also be included in the design of hardware, micro-controllers and embedded systems with their integrated and increasingly cryptographic processes?

Thanks to fast computing power, the cryptographic "chips" are faster than ever and also more mobile than ever.

With the smartphones, we hold small computers in our hands or in our pockets, which used to encompass several kilos or entire cupboards.

It is no longer just about becoming faster, smaller, more mobile, more trustworthy and more secure, but the software and hardware processes of a modern crypto-chip architecture are also to be adapted to the new requirements in accordance with the current Transformation of Cryptography.

Transferred to the hardware of Crypto-Chips and such secure embedded systems, the following potentials and questions can arise within this background:

- How can "Hearts" – Crypto-Chips – be linked with one another, also mobile and / or remotely, or at least communicate securely?

  If micro-processors are not just single (multiple) hearts within a single algorithm, Crypto-Chips can also be seen as independent entities and organisms within a network that connect like individual satellites of a peer-to-peer network, and are organized according to a division of labor with swarm intelligence? Or form a network that only transfers encrypted packets via the TCP / IP protocol?

- Will we soon have Crypto-Chips that can form a mesh or map defined routes in the sense of graph theory?

- How can hardware machines then automatically create and manage new neighbors and their encryption keys?

- Different Crypto-Chips could refer to different algorithms: e.g. if multi-encryption of ciphertext of one algorithm is repeated with another, different algorithm?

- Why shouldn't a Crypto-Chip take on the task of a packet check as we know it from a router or deep packet inspection (König 2013), filtering out duplicates and double packets, checking signatures or cryptographic tokens or the hash values provided?

- Or why shouldn't another chip dedicated as a Trusted Execution Environment take over the encryption and decryption processes (conversion) without the plaintext having to go through further layers at the application, keyboard driver or operating system level?

Driven by increasing digitization and the growing number of devices in the Internet of Things (IoT), we are currently experiencing great demand for such secure hardware-based solutions for machine to machine (M2M) authentication, cryptography and data typing, data protection, data forwarding and data storage.

The change in cryptography as well as the demand of the market, especially for example in the networking of technical household appliances, places the topic of secure embedded systems in the central focus of modern research and teaching.

The German Central Association for the Electrical and Electronics Industries (ZVEI - Zentralverband Elektrotechnik und Elektronikindustrie) even created a "National Roadmap Embedded Systems" (2016), of which the first and priority strategy is "seamless interaction", which would be unthinkable today without cryptography in the area of secure embedded systems.

Thomas Wollinger et. al. already predicted at the "Embedded World - Exhibition and Conference" in 2003: "Thus, it is our view that designing and implementing efficient cryptographic algorithms on embedded systems will continue to be an active research area."

Around 20 years later, with the Internet of Things, the fact that chips communicate with chips securely - washing machine to tablet like Alexa Echo-Dot to Alexa Echo-Dot - is virtually pandemic.

A publication by the IEEE by Pádraig Flood and Michael Schukat estimated "50 billion Internet-enabled devices" for 2020. A new Business Insider Intelligence study predicts even that the IoT market will grow 2025 to "more than 64 billion IoT devices" (Newman 2019).

We therefore see the explanations summarized in this essay, the references to the current Transformation of Cryptography, and the design draft to relate the referenced Echo protocol to the architecture and processes of a micro-controller as a basic element in the training of developers of micro-processors and in the teaching of the basics of cryptography and the security of embedded systems.

The further development of Crypto-Chips has been going on for many decades; however, it is currently facing new challenges that arise from the Transformation of Cryptography and the (secure) connection of hardware chips to hardware chips in a secure network.

In the following, we want to analyze these relationships as examples for cryptography in the field of mobile messaging based on the Echo protocol. It is ideal for exploring further models, findings and research needs in the contexts mentioned above and their intersections.

3 The Echo Protocol: Networking Encrypting Devices

So what does a microprocessor architecture look like that can map the encrypting and routing respective forwarding character of the Echo protocol?

Let us first describe the basics of the Echo encryption protocol.

The Echo Protocol was conceived around 2012 and published in the middle of 2013 in the software Spot-On Encryption Suite (Edwards / et al. 2019) and in the GoldBug Messenger GUI (Adams / Maier 2016) as a customized user interface for Echo kernels.

Spot-On is an open source software for encryption that enables e-mail, chat, file transfer and web search in a URL database in addition to other cryptographic functions and tools.

The software shows numerous innovations in the cryptographic and graph-theoretical field such as Cryptographic Calling, Secret Streams, the setting of Gold Bugs (passwords on e-mails) or the "Patch Points" for "private application pass thoughts" - a kind VPN tunnel for applications connected via the local host, which due to a traditional program code alone do not yet have encryption and which can establish the encrypted connection via the Spot-On Encryption Suite software (even with the McEliece algorithm).

GoldBug (instead of: Gold Bug) is a further design of a user interface that is adapted to a messenger in chat style and can also address every echo kernel or messenger server (listener) (Adams / Maier 2016). The name is reminiscent of Edgar Allan Poe, who described a cryptogram in his short story of the same name.

The Spot-On software is written in C++ and compatible with the Smoke Chat Messenger software written in Java for Android with the SmokeStack Android server, which, among other things, established the cryptographic innovation of Fiasco Forwarding with the Fiasco Keys (as a further development of the Signal Protocol) and the key transport problem solved with Secret Streams and the Juggernaut Keys. Cryptographic Discovery is also integrated in this server (see Smoke Technical Documentation 2019).

The basis of C++ as well as Java software is the Echo protocol, which can be characterized as follows:

Basically, every message sent, every packet sent, is encrypted within the Echo protocol. This can also be done by multi-encryption, i.e. ciphertext is converted into ciphertext once again using another algorithm.

Second: In principle, every packet is forwarded from a node to all the neighbors connected in the network.

As a third criterion for the Echo, the so-called echo match is defined as follows: the ciphertext converted back by a key is hashed and compared with the enclosed hash of the original message. If both hashes match, the correct key has been used for decoding and the conversion of ciphertext to plaintext can be read successfully by the user (see Gasakis / Schmidt 2018).

Hybrid multi-encryption is another outstanding innovation of the Echo: Multi-encryption means multiple encryption on different levels: The authors Linda Bertram and Gunther van Dooble (2019) write:

"Applied programming of hybrid encryption (means in the end that different variants are used at the same time or one after the other) finally led this theoretical and so far little-studied concept of Multi-Encryption with its variety of options into practical application processes. It is with the Multi-Encryption not only about encrypting a ciphertext again.

It's also about possibly changing the algorithm of encryption in the second round. While an algorithm knows several rounds, operations, repetitions of e.g. substitutions, multi-encryption now puts a whole new dimension on top of it: If plaintext has been converted to a ciphertext with the RSA algorithm, and this is then converted to another ciphertext by the McEliece algorithm: What comes out at the end? And can this be better or worse analyzed using the usual methods of cryptanalysis?

It is no longer just a question of substituting individual characters, but a completely new (second) algorithm is applied to the ciphertext end product of a previously used algorithm. Multi-Encryption thus consists of three main areas: The multiple encryption (conversion from ciphertext to ciphertext), and secondly, a mixture of algorithms, to thirdly the mixture of methods, which could certainly also fall under algorithms, therefore we say: Process chains.

The mixture also of the transfer ways of the keys, for example, complements methodical and procedural the mixture of algorithms, because it is a difference whether RSA-AES-McEliece triple changed ciphertext is sent through a channel of a permanent key or is sent through the channel of a temporary key."

The open-source software Spot-On was the first software to enable playing with different encryption routines and a hybrid design of symmetrical and asymmetrical encryption with different algorithms at the same time.

The Echo protocol also combines encryption with the graph theory: The authors Mele Gasakis and Max Schmidt (2018) explain that it is not a matter of routing, but the forwarding of packets is "beyond cryptographic routing", since each packet is quasi passed on to all neighbors without any destination information.

Because - according to the second Echo principle - a packet is basically forwarded to all connected neighbors. This also makes it more difficult to record metadata in the network (according to the analysis question: who communicates with whom and when).

However, message packets that are sent from one node to all connected further nodes have a great chance of passing another node again.

In order to exclude known packets of messages from a second inspection by an echo kernel, they are hashed and compared with the list of known hashes. This is known as "Congestion Control" (Nomenclatura 2019).

Messages that have already passed the node can thus be identified and the burden of forwarding or inspecting the packets as to whether they can be opened with a key can be reduced.

These elements mentioned would be essential for the Echo protocol and an implementation in a micro-controller - as a hardware solution would at least have to take these protocol and cryptography-oriented processes into account in an architectural design.

In addition, other aspects can be mentioned:

The previous software architecture relates to a user interface and a kernel. In the Spot-On Encryption Suite, this is programmed in the C++ language and the server is defined as a listener in the user interface.

Furthermore, a header-less server Spot-on-Lite is available, which can be configured only using a console without a user interface.

For the Java implementation in the area of the SmokeStack server, further functionalities are implemented e.g. to operate as a key server for the Android client Smoke.

This server can therefore store keys such as the 100 times larger keys of the McEliece algorithm (with 0.3 MB instead of 400 bytes of the RSA key) and then offer them to new users.

Since the key is only exchanged once, if no further ephemeral (temporary) Fiasco keys are used with this algorithm, the effort compared to the RSA key, which is now considered insecure (see NIST 2016), remains only episodic and therefore justifiable.

Furthermore, the SmokeStack Server also offers postbox functions for the retrieval of offline messages in the area of messaging (chat / e-mail).

With the Steam protocol (implemented in Java in the smoke client) and the StarBeam protocol (implemented in the C++ programming of the Spot-On Encryption Suite), a TCP-like design of return information about the receipt of a package is implemented on the basis of the Echo protocol.

"Steam" and "StarBeam" are compatible with each other (Nomenclatura 2019; Smoke 2020). This means that TCP runs on the completely encrypted layer of the Echo protocol. The Echo thus has the potential to replace TCP based on TCP and to implement a fully encrypted network protocol.

For the operational part of the key management, reference should also be made to the EPKS protocol (see Spot-On 2012, Edwards 2019): Echo Public Key Sharing, in which a new key exchange or a new listener / server as information is sent to other instances, which can be processed automatically or via a notification in a user interface for the respective hardware chip. This means that the part of the key- and neighbor/server-management is also addressed on the protocol side.

The function, which is later called AutoCrypt in other implementations, goes back to the EPKS function (see Nomenclatura 2019).

An implementation of all these functions is now to be discussed for the design of a micro-controller architecture: How can a micro-controller or how can microprocessors map and / or support parts or entire processes of these functionalities that were previously designed in the software?

4   Hardware Architecture

The further considerations for the design of a future development of Crypto-Chips in the area of secure communication should initially be based on a very basic starting point: Cryptographic processes of communication, or also the encoding of speech in telephone calls, take place today on mobile phones.

With numerous Android and proportionately fewer Apple / iOS devices for both operating systems, a quasi 80/20 monoculture has established: These two monopolistic providers can hardly escape a person who wants to communicate mobile and digitally. The data and communication of life must be entrusted to one of the two providers.

It is becoming increasingly clear that smartphones are also made to collect and consolidate user data for commercial and monitoring purposes.

With this combination of mobile hardware and software, the user is a transparent consumer: "Google data is the new gold", Jörg Forthmann (2016) summarizes the systematic sniffing out on smartphones.

But it's not just about aggregated data being used as big data, but that these operating systems appear to be designed to have explicit back doors so that individual users can be addressed, and text entries copied and uploaded before an encryption process: "Big Data" is supplemented by "Data OutFlow by Design".

How can encryption still be considered secure if every non-open-source process step in software and in the operating system in general has to be evaluated as potentially a Trojan and "backdoor in spé" - or at least as a dual-use function:

- It becomes interesting if the respective American manufacturer of the operating system fears that a Chinese application will process user data - and not just the American system or its applications: "Data Outflow" has become a national question. *(Considering this background, it should be noted that the Spot-On Encryption Suite is open-source and therefore not only remains independent of national interests, but also does not know any central servers that could aggregate user data. The possibility of having an own, self-hosted open-source Echo Server operated is a crucial security feature to prevent data outflow).*

- Even if a PDF has been sent from one Android user to another Android user via an end-to-end encrypted channel and the user opens the PDF on their end device in another application, this application can send a copy of the document to a central server and compromise the content of the document. Or if the browser offers an account-based translation of a web document, read content can be reviewed centrally as a copy. The view right of personally delivered, confidential documents has become divisible on smartphones and the own sovereignty of a cognitive process can be controlled by others. *(Considering this background, all transferred attachments of the Smoke Crypto Chat Messenger, for example, are stored in an encrypted database and are only displayed by the Smoke software. For processing in other applications, it must first be exported and saved as a plain attachment, - using password-based user authentication).*

- In these cases, the security of the architecture on such a device is just as bad as if a sender is already given text components of his message to a central point when entering a text message via the keyboard: be it e.g. through the spell check, for "improvement purposes of the user experience" or even by a state Trojan. Texts to be encrypted are ideally copied by Trojans where they are entered as plaintext: in the layer of the keyboard. *(To prevent this, for example, the GoldBug Messenger has a virtual keyboard with which only mouse clicks can be listened to, but not the login password).*

[At the end of this book, we take up these and other risk cases again with an evaluation of how an encryption chip to be developed can provide hardware perspectives in this context and which other research questions arise from these contexts].

In short, smart mobile devices - especially those with an Android or Apple operating system - are not safe on the hardware and software today, but open like a barn door: "Data Outflow by Design".
According to the formulation of the new paradigm, so-called "Trusted Execution Environments" (TEE) are required, which are separated as a Secure Embedded System, for plaintext input and encryption and decryption processes (which we also refer to as "conversion") - to be kept secret.

Hardware-based "Trusted Execution Environments" will play a more dedicated role in the architectural design of secure embedded systems in the future.

4.1 Cryptographic Conversions on Secure Embedded Systems

Modern embedded systems are often based on micro-controllers (i.e. microprocessors with integrated memory and peripheral interfaces), but ordinary microprocessors (using external chips for memory and peripheral interface circuits) are also common, especially in more complex systems. In either case, the processors used may be types ranging from general purpose to those specialized in certain class of computations.

Embedded systems thus represent a combination of hardware and software components that are integrated in a technical context and have the task of controlling, regulating or monitoring a system.

Secure Embedded Systems perform security-related and cryptographic tasks.

An (secure) embedded system therefore performs predefined, dedicated tasks, often with real-time calculation requirements. In contrast, a conventional computer can perform many different tasks depending on the software used.

Aligning the micro-controllers for a dedicated purpose (such as the encryption processes of converting) frees them from the range of other tasks and the associated security risks.

These micro-controllers are mostly programmed in the programming languages assembler, C or C++. 32-bit architectures are predominantly programmed in these high-level languages. However, other languages such as BASIC, Pascal, Forth or Ada are also used.

The German Federal Association for Information Technology, Telecommunications and New Media (BITKOM - Bundesverband Informationswirtschaft, Telekommunikation und neue Medien) (2010) sees priority fields of application for embedded systems in the following areas: For example, the ignition control of airbags in the automotive industry, ABS systems, public transport, modern office and communication electronics, energy technology, mobile phones, infotainment. Industrial automation, medical technology, telecommunications systems, military technology, household appliances or security technology.

None of these application areas can do without cryptography of the Secure Embedded Systems.

The development of a USB stick with cryptographic functions towards business maturity can be cited as an already historical, simple example of storing or also transporting and transferring content worth protecting: the Nitro Key.

4.2 Example: NitroKey

In 2008 Jan Suhr, Rudolf Böddeker and another friend were traveling and found themselves looking to use encrypted e-mails in Internet cafés, which meant the secret keys had to remain secure against computer viruses.

Some proprietary USB dongles existed at the time, but lacked in certain ways. Consequentially, they established an open source project which grew under the name NitroKey.

It was a spare-time project of the founders to develop a hardware solution to enable the secure usage of e-mail encryption. The first version of the Crypto Stick was released 2009. In late 2014 the founders decided to professionalize the project.

NitroKey's firmware was audited by German cybersecurity firm Cure53 in May 2015 (Heiderich 2015), and its hardware was audited by the same company in August 2015 (Nedospasov 2015). The first four NitroKey models became available in September of the same year.

This example shows that with a little self-initiative, with friends and years of hard work on the same topic context, productive results can be achieved and corresponding initiatives in the field of hardware production are not only to be classified as university exams.

Even if no one can use a chip factory to create a micro-controller, today, however, corresponding single-board controllers and computers offer the possibility of having own programming carried out on these boards - similar to what happens in a student project with the NitroKey has begun.

For example, Raspberry Pi and Arduino make it possible to deal with Secure Embedded Systems at an early stage in appropriate learning environments and to come to your own results with cryptographic processes installed on hardware.

Today the micro SD card "Crypto Mobile HC-9100" can do infinitely more: With it you have "the smallest high-security encryption platform in the world", writes Crypto International AG (compare von Matt / Schmid 2020) and also the "IronKey D300" as USB-Stick is much more advanced (Kingsley-Hughes 2020).

4.3 Example: Arduino & Raspberry Pi

Arduino is an open-source hardware and software company, project and user community that designs and manufactures single-board micro-controllers and micro-controller kits for building digital devices.

Its products are licensed under the GNU Lesser General Public License (LGPL) or the GNU General Public License (GPL), permitting the manufacture of Arduino boards and software distribution by anyone.

A program for Arduino hardware may be written in any programming language with compilers that produce binary machine code for the target processor. The Arduino IDE supports the languages C and C++ using special rules of code structuring (Purdum 2012). Also the Raspberry Pi micro-controller is an adequate development platform to design a cryptographically secure chip-set (Molloy 2016, Tomar 2020).

These two single-board platforms are the best known, with which developers can learn the design of a micro-controller for cryptographic processes and program a secure embedded system with little effort.

These two single-board platforms are the best known, so how would such a plan have to be defined in the design for different security zones in order to be able to cover the Transformation aspects of Cryptography as well as the basic routines of the encrypting Echo protocol in the architectural design layout?

4.4 Defining the architectural Design of Echo on a Chip (EoC)

While numerous use cases only involve the secure connection or networking of devices, telecommunications are particularly concerned with the content of the messages to be transmitted that is worthy of trust and protection (even over several hops). Secure embedded systems in the area of networked messaging and telecommunications are therefore of particular importance.

In the field of mobile telecommunications, however, no user will be able to purchase a new smartphone with every chip audited and secured. The hardware is also dependent on the data operating mobile operating systems and their layers, as shown above.

Encryption can therefore only be carried out securely by programming own open source hardware and software on Secure Embedded Systems - and / or: One separates the vulnerable hardware - that wants to send out data - from the rest of the network.

The idea of securing the conversion of the encryption process on a Trusted Execution Environment is just as central as the practice of being able to write and make phone calls in encrypted form via an own, self-hosted server.

Using our example of the encryption process based on the Echo protocol, it would make sense to enter the text or a voice message and encrypt it on a micro-controller device that is not connected to the Internet or to a public network.

The Echo capsule, consisting of the encrypted ciphertext and the enclosed hash of the original message, is created on this device and then exported as an encrypted capsule. This capsule can then be transported to a device (e.g. by changing to another protocol that is free of TCP) and given to the regular TCP network at that other node for forwarding. This means that the encryption capsule is packaged separately before shipping. We will specify this idea in detail below as Echo Chip # 1.

For decryption, it is necessary to check how many packets pass the node, whether they can be buffered and should also be routed to a TEE via a non-IP-bound transport to be defined.[1]

By changing the protocol from the regular node integrated into the IP network to the TEE, it can still be assumed that an attacker cannot inject Trojans or malware. It is unlikely that a Trojan will be smuggled into a node via TCP, which will then unfold further into the next node via Bluetooth. Even if the paradigm of changing the protocol no longer works, there is the option of leaving the TEE offline and

---

[1] The Echo protocol offers flexibility here: a so-called half echo can be defined: With Half Echo, the packets are only forwarded one hop from the sender to the server and then to the recipient - and not beyond that. In this respect, the graph design that can be influenced in the Echo protocol also influences the packet volume in the network and thus offers the opportunity to trigger the work processes for decoding on a "Trusted Execution Environment" (Echo chip #1) in relation to the node that is regularly connected with Full Echo to the network.

transmitting encrypted packets via USB if the USB stick remains sterile, i.e. used once and then formatted or renewed.

For example, regular nodes of the Echo can be connected via TCP on the Internet, and a TEE can then also be connected via a UDP or Bluetooth listener - if you do not want to manually transfer the encrypted Echo capsule with an USB stick from the separated TEE to the regular Echo node and add it to an open listener.

In any case, with a TEE that is not connected to the network, is quasi virgin and original, and the encryption processes take over, there are only very limited possibilities to monitor it. In the same manner, a deciphering TEE can be created for encrypted packets that can be taken off from the network.

From a cryptographic point of view, nodes located on the Internet (with mobile devices) must be regarded as contaminated for plaintext input.[2]

Encryption and decryption processes should take place on a separate station to keep contamination free: However, this means fundamentally in the hardware design that transport nodes must be separated from nodes that encrypt or decipher;

---

[2] If the internet and its connected mobile devices are regarded as contaminated, is then a separation (or even an isolation) of the process of plaintext conversion sufficient, as it would be the case in medical quarantine measures for SARS or corona COVID-19 virus infections 10-14 days before symptom detection (Cohen 2020)? The research question transferred from medicine would be then: How can a quarantine for encryption and decryption processes be walled?

just as kernel processes and processes of the user interface are often separated in the software mapping and are only connected as required using suitable methods.

Finally, there is always the possibility of operating an Echo Server behind an Echo Server as a relay, the connection of which is then secured to the trusted execution environment (Echo Client = TCP => Echo Server = TCP => Echo Server = Bluetooth => Echo Chip #1).

Furthermore, Crypto-Chips can also take over tasks of a node located on the Internet (Echo Chip #2), for example to route or respective forward packets, or to perform the function of congestion control. To do this, it is necessary to use a cache in which the hashes of the packets passing by are temporarily stored.

Likewise, these Crypto-Chips could also be connected to one another as nodes, either that they can be found independently within a local network, or else through a listener broadcast via the Echo connection itself.

The programming of an Echo Server with extended server functions such as key management or mailbox functionalities would then involve an Echo Chip #3.

For single-board computers, such programming can be based on the C++ language - or also in the Java language: program code from the existing software Spot-On, Spot-on-Lite, Smoke and SmokeStack is available for both languages.

The design of the security architecture proposed here provides for three different micro-controllers:

- Separated Secure Embedded System / Crypto-Controller 1: A Trusted Execution Environment without a connection to the Internet for converting the plaintext to ciphertext and vice versa. The encrypted Echo capsule is packaged here.
- Secure Embedded System / Crypto-Controller 2: Internet server (listener) for connecting clients and as a mirror / forwarder of message packets according to the Echo protocol to all connected neighbors.
- Secure Embedded System / Crypto-Controller 3: A key server with a post-box function.

The two Crypto-Chips on the Internet and the non-Internet connected Trusted Execution Environment can be graphically depicted as follows:

Figure 1: Echo on a Chip (Three Designs for Cryptographic Micro-Controllers based on the Echo Protocol)

Figure 1: Echo on a Chip - 3 Designs for Cryptographic Micro-Controllers based on the Echo Protocol

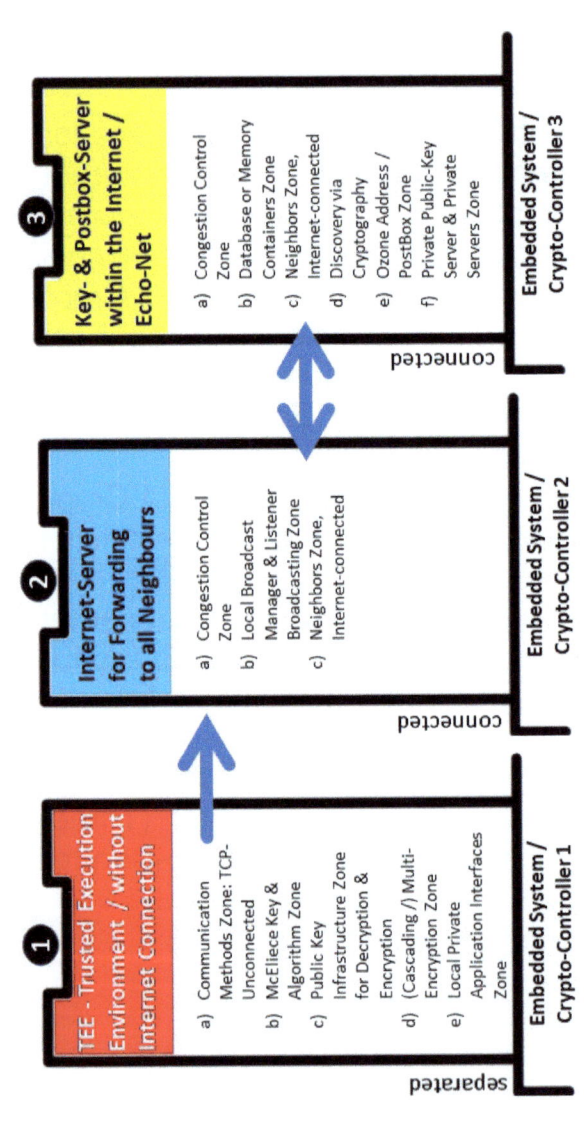

Echo on a Chip (EoC)

A New Perception for the Next Generation of Micro-Controllers as Separated Secure Embedded Systems (SSES) handling Multi-Encryption

1 — **TEE - Trusted Execution Environment / without Internet Connection**

a) Communication Methods Zone: TCP-Unconnected
b) McEliece Key & Algorithm Zone
c) Public Key Infrastructure Zone for Decryption & Encryption
d) (Cascading /) Multi-Encryption Zone
e) Local Private Application Interfaces Zone

Embedded System / Crypto-Controller 1

separated

2 — **Internet-Server for Forwarding to all Neighbours**

a) Congestion Control Zone
b) Local Broadcast Manager & Listener Broadcasting Zone
c) Neighbors Zone, Internet-connected

Embedded System / Crypto-Controller 2

connected

3 — **Key- & Postbox-Server within the Internet / Echo-Net**

a) Congestion Control Zone
b) Database or Memory Containers Zone
c) Neighbors Zone, Internet-connected
d) Discovery via Cryptography
e) Ozone Address / PostBox Zone
f) Private Public-Key Server & Private Servers Zone

Embedded System / Crypto-Controller 3

connected

40

5 Hardware Echo-Chip - Part # I - Encryption and Decryption Processes on a Trusted Execution Environment

The first Echo-Chip consists of the following different Zones to establish a Trusted Execution Environment:

- Communication Methods Zone
- McEliece Key & Algorithm Zone
- Public Key Infrastructure Zone
- Cascading / Multi-Encryption Zone
- Local Private Application Interfaces Zone

The Echo-Chip #1 is not connected to the regular Internet via the regular IP/TCP Protocol. On this chip text is entered and converted to ciphertext (or speech is converted to ciphertext).

As a quantum computing resistant algorithm the McEliece Algorithm will be used within the Public Key Infrastructure Zone.

Cascading / Multi-Encryption can be applied, that means a message can be first encrypted symmetrically e.g. with AES and then again converted with the McEliece Algorithm Key asymmetrically.

After the conversion to an encrypted packet has been taken place, the transport is constructed not over a regular TCP/IP-connection: e.g. a protocol change to e.g. Bluetooth or the export via an USB

41

Stick makes sense, so that taping or coping of the plaintext is not possible without further means.

Also, the function of a Local Private Application Interfaces allows an application to use two Echo-Chips #1 to act like a VPN to secure the connection even for applications, which have no encryption.

The individual requirements for these five Zones can be detailed out based on the Spot-On Software with the following specifications:

5.1 Communication Methods Zone: TCP-Disconnected Communication Methods via Protocol-Change, e.g. Bluetooth or UDP

Spot-On – or the Communication Methods Zone on Echo Chip #1 needs to – supports Bluetooth, SCTP, TCP, and UDP (multicast and unicast) communication methods. Both, IPv4 and IPv6, are totally supported. Some communications portions also support a variety of proxies. For TCP-based and UDP-based unicast communications, OpenSSL is supported. Spot-On distributes data with or without SSL/TLS. In essence, the application is generally transport-neutral.

Please note that Bluetooth and SCTP support require operating system support. Here this might be an option to change the protocol and to disconnect the Trusted Execution Environment from the Internet, though the transport mechanism still needs some further elaboration and research to prevent that infiltrating incoming packets destroy the Trusted

Execution Environment. The Echo Chip # 1 needs to be not monitored as it fulfills the role to convert plaintext entries to an encrypted packet (and vice versa).

5.2 McEliece Key & Algorithm Zone

Echo-Chip #1 integrates an independent and self-contained classical McEliece implementation as the model is given with the Spot-On software. The implementation is there based on the software and writings of McEliece (1978), Preneel et al. (1992), Roering (2013), Repka (2014).

Some general information: Spot-On supports m value 11 and t value 51. For m = 11 and t = 51, k = 1487 and n = 2048. As a result, the message expansion factor is approximately 1.4. Parameters m = 12 and t = 68 are also provided.

A private key consists of matrices P-1 and S-1, the code support L, a binary irreducible Goppa polynomial g, and a vector. The matrices contain 2048 x 2048 and 1487 x 1487 entries, respectively. The polynomial contains 51 entries. The vector contains 2048 entries. A total of 6,407,572 entries are required.

A public key consists of matrix Ĝ and t. A total of 1487 x 2048, or 3,045,376, entries are required.

Included is an interpretation, model a, of the Fujisaki-Okamoto conversion (compare Hudde 2013): The key streams are generated via single-round PBKDF2 and SHA-256. The generated 32-

byte salts are transferred as clear text. Computation errors abort the processes.

Decryption

1. Decipher, via McEliece, c1 to obtain the original message m.
2. Compute the original error vector e via e = c1 − m * $\hat{G}$.
3. Compute the SHA-256 digest of e.
4. Apply the previously-computed digest to a single round of the PBKDF2 function. The generated key stream, k2, will contain 1488 bits of which the first 1487 will be consumed in the following computation. The 32-byte salt, s2, is provided to PBKDF2.
5. Compute mcar = c2 xor k2.
6. Compute the SHA-256 digest of e || mcar.
7. Apply the previously-computed digest to a single round of the PBKDF2 function. The generated key stream, k1, will contain 1488 bits of which the first 1487 will be consumed in the following computation. The 32-byte salt, s1, is provided to PBKDF2.
8. Verify that c1 = k1 * $\hat{G}$ + e.

Encryption

1. Generate a random vector e of length n. The vector e will contain t randomly-dispersed ones.
2. Compute the SHA-256 digest of e || m, where m is the original message.
3. Apply the previously-computed digest to a single round of the PBKDF2 function. The generated key stream, k1, will contain 1488 bits of which the first 1487 will be consumed in the following computation. A 32-byte weakly-derived salt, s1, is provided to PBKDF2.
4. Compute $c1 = k1 * \hat{G} + e$.
5. Compute the SHA-256 digest of e.
6. Apply the previously-computed digest to a single round of the PBKDF2 function. The generated key stream, k2, will contain 1488 bits of which the first 1487 will be consumed in the following computation. A 32-byte weakly-derived salt, s2, is provided to PBKDF2.
7. Compute $c2 = k2$ xor m.
8. Transfer c1, c2, s1, and s2.

Included is an interpretation, model b, of the Fujisaki-Okamoto conversion (compare Hudde 2013): The key streams are generated via SHAKE-256. libgcrypt 1.7.0 or newer is required. Computation errors abort the processes.

Decryption

1. Decipher, via McEliece, c1 to obtain the original message m.
2. Compute the original error vector e via $e = c1 - m * \hat{G}$.
3. Compute the SHAKE-256 digest of e. The generated key stream, k2, will contain 1488 bits of which the first 1487 will be consumed in the following computation.
4. Compute mcar = c2 xor k2.
5. Compute the SHAKE-256 digest of e || mcar. The generated key stream, k1, will contain 1488 bits of which the first 1487 will be consumed in the following computation.
6. Verify that $c1 = k1 * \hat{G} + e$.

Encryption

1. Generate a random vector e of length n. The vector e will contain t randomly-dispersed ones.
2. Compute the SHAKE-256 digest of e || m, where m is the original message. The generated key stream, k1, will contain 1488 bits of which the first 1487 will be consumed in the following computation.

3. Compute $c_1 = k_1 * \hat{G} + e$.
4. Compute the SHAKE-256 digest of e. The generated key stream, k_2, will contain 1488 bits of which the first 1487 will be consumed in the following computation.
5. Compute $c_2 = k_2$ xor m.
6. Transfer c_1 and c_2.

Please note, that the Java implementation of the McEleice algorithm within the Smoke Chat Messenger, which is the first quantum computing resistant McEliece-Messenger worldwide, also includes a third model, c, for a Pointcheval Modulus (11, 50).

Screenshot I: Smoke Crypto Chat Messenger

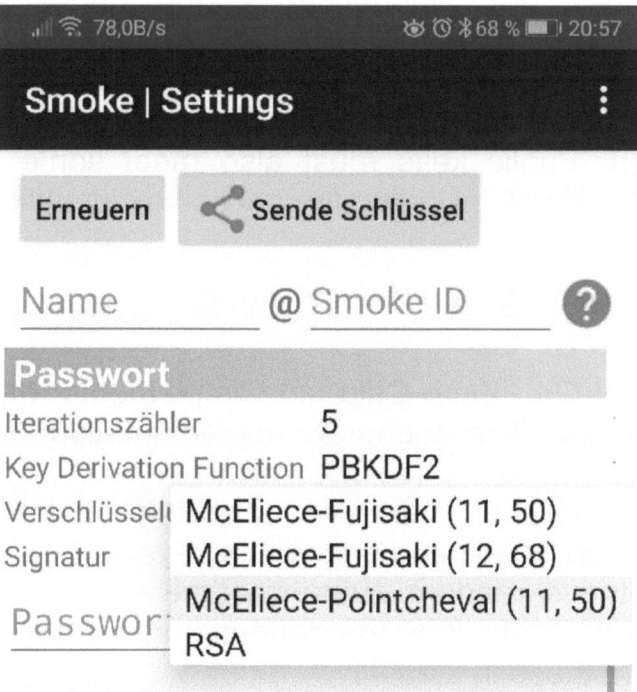

5.3 Public Key Infrastructure Zone
for Decryption & Encryption

As Spot-On, Echo-Chip #1 utilizes the libgcrypt and libntru libraries for permanent private and public key pairs. Key generation is optional. Consequently, it does not require a public key infrastructure.

ElGamal, McEliece, NTRU, and RSA encryption algorithms are supported. DSA, ECDSA, EdDSA, ElGamal, and RSA signature algorithms are supported. The OAEP and PSS schemes are used with RSA encryption and RSA signing, respectively.

Communications between nodes having diverse key types are well-defined if the nodes share common libgcrypt and libntru libraries.

Non-McEliece and Non-NTRU private keys are evaluated for correctness via the gcry_pk_testkey() function. Public keys must also meet some basic criteria such as including the public-key identifier.

5.4 Cascading / Multi-Encryption

As Spot-On, Echo-Chip #1, implements multiple encryption. The general implementation is as follows:
1. If available, retrieve previously-established authentication and encryption keys.
2. Retrieve random authentication and encryption keys. Verify that the random credentials differ from those in step #1.

3. Generate a hybrid bundle: RSA(#2) || AES(message) || HMAC(RSA(#2) || AES(message)). Some variations are also possible. Camelia, Gost, Serpent, Threefish, and Twofish cipher algorithms are supported. As for digest algorithms, SHA, Stribog, and Whirlpool are included.
4. Generate a bundle from the data in step #3 using the keys from step #1: AES(#3) || HMAC(AES(#3)).
5. If SSL/TLS is available, funnel the bundle from step #4 through the SSL/TLS layer.

5.5 Local Private Application Interfaces

As Spot-On, Echo-Chip #1, supports the concept of local private application interfaces. The interfaces allow networked applications to stream authenticated and encrypted data through a Echo network. Application-native cryptographic capabilities are not required. A local listener, such as 127.0.0.1:4710, should be defined per application. Once defined, credentials may be prepared for the listener.

Let's exercise:
1. Decide on the interface of the application. That is, Bluetooth, TCP, etc. Does it require SSL/TLS?
2. Create a local private listener, say 127.0.0.1:4710.

3. Enable the pass-through setting on the listener.
4. Prepare the pseudo-private credentials via a context menu.
5. Distribute the credentials to your partners. Remember, these are not necessarily private credentials. However, let's consider them as such.
6. Initiate the kernel process.
7. Connect your application to the previously-defined listener.

Do remember that if this process is on a public network, data will arrive through the public interface(s). However, your networked application will only receive applicable data; that is, data that was encapsulated by your credentials. As we consider the Echo-Chip #1 to be a Trusted Execution Environment, streaming will have special requirements to connect the encrypting/decryption chip with the regular Internet respectively an Echo Listener on the regular Internet without endangering the Trust of this entering pad or chip.

Spot-On as software guarantees ordered data delivery for Local Private Application Interfaces, and so should the design of an Echo-Chip #1 as a Trusted Execution Environment.
    After this Encryption (Decryption) pad or chip has done its work, it is about to deliver the encrypted packet to an Echo Server (Listener) within the regular Internet connected to other Echo nodes on the Internet. The encrypted packet is over-given and

now the forwarding – not to say the routing – of the packet takes place. This will be done by the design of an Echo Chip #2, which is the correspondent of a Spot-On Software based Server or Listener.

6 Hardware Echo-Chip - Part # II - Meshing the Flood: Implementing Routing and Graph Theory into Hardware

The Echo Chip # 2 implements in its design an Forwarding Server. Each arriving Packet at this node is multiplied to all connected neighbors or clients.
This chip consists of the following zones:
- Congestion Control Zone
- Local Broadcast Manager & Listener Broadcasting Zone
- Neighbors Zone

The specific requirements of these zone can be described as follows in detail:

6.1 Congestion Control Zone

The Echo-Chip #2 implements a software-based congestion control mechanism.

As described, the Echo sends each packet always to all connected neighbors, hence in an Echo Network a packet might come back to a node via other neighbors. Congestion control identifies these packets via hashing and prevents the need to inspect or to forward the packet once again.

As within the Smoke Chat Echo Java Software, the SipHash algorithm could be used for computing digests. Computed digests are stored in an SQLite database table, respective a writable memory space of the micro-controller. Congestion control items could be inspected every 5 seconds. Items older than 60 seconds could be discarded.

6.2 Local Broadcast Manager & Listener Broadcasting Zone

For the software part, communications between an Echo-Kernel and the user interface utilize a Local Broadcast Manager instance.

Also there is a Listener Broadcasting process. As it is not necessary a requirement, that the forwarding (quasi aka routing) server needs to have a graphical user interface, the automatism could be used, that over the Echo network announced new neighbors or new server listeners could be connected automatically. That might be regarded as an aspect of sovereignty to prevent other nodes from connecting or as a privilege, to manually decide which other nodes connect. But as all is encrypted and one Echo-Chip #2 should be able to automatically connect to another Echo-Chip #2 – if announced over the Internet connection, one might get rid of the risks appearing when a local broadcast manager connects a graphical user interface automatically.

This design balance needs to be further discussed: either if a manual steering within an Echo packet forwarding node (consolidated on a hardware micro-controller.) over a graphical user interface is more risky - or a micro-controller. having no graphical interface, but then is auto-connecting every node appearing to this chip over the established connection (Listener Broadcast).

6.3 Neighbors Zone

Neighbors may be defined also via the user interface or they are automatically accepted over the Echo neighbor broadcasting mechanism.

The software implementation offers infinitely-many IPv4 and IPv6 TCP and UDP client definitions. Each network peer includes dedicated and independent data-parsing, socket-reading, and socket-writing tasks. TCP neighbors support HTTP and SOCKS proxies. Please note that host translations are not performed via assigned proxies.

For the Echo-Chip #2 with these aforementioned zones the basic Echo principle needs to be operated, that once inserted encrypted Echo-Packets are forwarded at this listener- or server-node to all connected other nodes or neighbors.

Hence, the Echo-Chip #2 is a kind of "forwarder", to not to say a kind of "router" – considering that the Echo is "Beyond Cryptographic Routing" as above explained and referenced to Gasakis/Schmidt (2018).

This Echo-Chip #2 is connected within the regular Internet.

7   Hardware Echo-Chip - Part # III - Key Servers & Ozone Postbox Functionalities

Echo-Chip #1 is encrypting the plaintext to an encrypted capsule; and this capsule leaves over to be defined transport the Trusted Execution Environment and is inserted into the regular Echo Network over the Listener of Echo-Chip #2, which forwards as a server the multiplied capsule to all connected neighbors.

Echo-Chip #3 now extends then the Echo Server functionalities as a kind of key server and postbox for offline messages, as it is in software given within the SmokeStack Echo Server (programmed in Java).

The different zones and functionalities of this Echo-Chip #3 consists of:

7.1 Congestion Control Zone

This zone of Echo-Chip #3 has the same functionality as described for zone 6.1 of Echo-Chip #2: It is a Congestion Control Zone.

7.2 Database or Memory Containers Zone

Next to the described memory zone for congestion control hashes, this Echo Chip #3 needs also some database containers or memory space to store data regarding the functionality of providing a key server and/or a postbox for messages, which are saved for users, who are currently offline. Most of the database fields contain here authentically-encrypted values. Some fields contain keyed digests, including keyed digests of binary (false / true) values. Values are stored as E(Data, Ke) || HMAC(E(Data, Ke), Ka) and HMAC(Data, Ka). 256-bit AES-CBC is used for encrypting data. SHA-512 HMAC is used for data authentication.

7.3 Neighbors Zone

For sure, this Key-/Postbox-Server of Echo-Chip #3 needs also to be connected within the regular Internet to an Echo-Neighbor. Neighbors may be defined as described in the Zone 6.3 for Echo Chip #2.

7.4 Discovery via Cryptography

Cryptographic Discovery is a mechanism which allows servers to lighten the computational and data responsibilities of mobile devices. Cryptographic Discovery has been described by Gasakis/Schmidt (2018) and is programmed in the Smoke Crypto Chat Application in Java: Shortly after a Smoke instance connects to a SmokeStack service, the Smoke instance shares some non-private material. The material allows a SmokeStack server to transfer messages to their correct destinations. To mitigate replay attacks, Smoke instances offer SmokeStack instances random identity streams during message-retrieval requests. The identity streams self-expire.

The Echo-Chip #3 could implement this functionality accordingly into its design via an Cryptographic Discovery (CD) Zone.

7.5 Ozone Address / PostBox Zone

An Ozone address is a pseudo-private string which identifies a virtual entity. In software, Smoke Chat and SmokeStack Server utilize Ozones as a means of retrieving and storing offline messages and public-key pairs. If an Ozone address is defined and the network is available, in software the Smoke Chat Client will request external messages once per minute. Smoke Chat Client supports one Ozone while SmokeStack Server supports infinitely many.

An Ozone address must be exchanged separately. It is possible for multiple Smoke parties to house distinct Ozones if common SmokeStack instances are aware of the distinct Ozone addresses.[3]

---

[3] *Initialize Ozone:* If enabled, the Ozone credentials will be generated from the specified neighbor values. For example, let's suppose that a SmokeStack is attached to the service bee.service.org:4710. When preparing the neighbor information in Smoke Chat Client using the aforementioned SmokeStack destination, the Ozone will be initialized to bee.service.org:4710:TCP. In SmokeStack, the Ozone bee.service.org:4710:TCP should also be defined. This means,

The Ozone PostBox functionality would be an adequate zone also for an Echo-Chip #3, though the messages to offline users in the Echo could also be steered over two other innovative ways within Echo Software clients (like Spot-On), e.g. over "E-Mail Institutions" (Nomenclatura 2019), or storing the messages in a third common friends while using Half Echo (direct one hop server connection) (compare also Spot-On Documentation 2011, Edwards et al. 2019).

7.6 Private Public-Key Server & Private Servers Zone

In addition to housing messages, the SmokeStack Server software also serves as a private public-key server. A SmokeStack administrator is responsible for coordinating the storage of public-key pairs of participants. Participants may request public-key pairs of specific participants via Ozone addresses.

SmokeStack supports furthermore the concept of private servers for TCP clients. A private server will disregard non-authentication data until a remote peer has been authenticated.

The authentication process is as follows:

---

an Ozone address may be assigned via a graphical user interface, which would be needed for this Ozone Zone of the Echo Crypto-Chip #3. When completed, the Smoke Client and SmokeStack Server instances are artificially paired.

1. A private server generates a 64-byte stream of random data and concatenates the data with the current system time.
2. The server submits the SHA-512 hash of the information generated in the previous step to the remote peer after the SSL/TLS handshake has been completed. The server will repeatedly submit unique information every 10 seconds until the peer has authenticated itself.
3. The remote peer retrieves a stream of 64 random bytes as well as its signature key digest. It digitally signs the 64 random bytes, the signature key digest, and the original stream of random data and submits the 64 random bytes, the signature key digest, and the digital signature to the remote server. Please note that SmokeStack servers are conceptually indistinguishable from one another. Therefore, remote peers do not provide SmokeStack identifiers during this step.
4. The server reviews the two random-byte streams for uniqueness. If the two byte streams are dissimilar, it validates the digital signature. If the digital signature is valid and the two random-byte streams are dissimilar, the remote peer is authenticated.

Please define private servers after the desired participants have been completely defined in SmokeStack. This is required because SmokeStack instances must be in possession of public-key pairs. Please note that multiple devices may contain identical Smoke instances. Thus, several identical Smoke instances may authenticate themselves with a given SmokeStack instance.

Such an Echo-Chip #3 with functionalities regarding key server services and Offline Message housing and regarding the routines of Cryptographic Discovery would be the third architecture we suggest to build into a third design of a micro-controller chip.

As said, all these functions are given in software. Either over the code of Spot-On or the code of Smoke and SmokeStack. The idea to implement a separated approach into these suggested secure embedded Systems broadens them with the approach to provide a Trusted Execution Environment towards a "Separated Secure Embedded System" paradigm, in short: SSES.

What provides such an Echo-Chip Design and the new approach of a "Separated Secure Embedded System" (SSES) regarding a separation of a Trusted Execution Environment for the actual discussion of risk cases? We want to mention seven of such risk cases and give some solution insight based on Echo and Cryptography on Chips with regard also to further research and development requirements.

8 Conclusions for contextual risk cases with research and development requirements

The above design draft for the development of Secure Embedded Systems with cryptography-capable chips and micro-controllers for dedicated and secured functions can show solutions that underline the need for further research even with current developments.

Current risk cases are currently to be named as follows, which will influence further development at various levels.

8.1 Risk Case: From ToTok to TikTok

It seems as if the Android operating system was developed in order to be able to upload and analyze user data and keyboard input at the level of the operating system and the individual applications. It is a platform for the best possible analysis of consumers (Schmidt 2012, Fairsearch 2013, Soghoian 2015, Holland 2018).

One example is the accusation against the China-based development company of the TikTok application, which is used to upload private data to Chinese exploitation purposes, so that the application was banned on smartphones from the U.S. government (Stanley 2019, Cox 2019).

What a miracle, not only American companies can upload user data with the mobile operating system and its landscape of applications, but also companies from world-wide countries like China.

Interestingly, the same case is running with the ToTok application, which sounds the same: The smartphone program was therefore used by the United Arab Emirates government to track every conversation, movement, connection, appointment, sound and image files of the users (Mazzetti et al . 2019).

Research and Development requirements:

Applications that send user data to manufacturers or government agencies are common today. The majority of users know little about the background processes, which of their data is transferred and how it is evaluated.

This applies in particular to closed source applications in which even developers cannot check the program code.

All the more, the paradigm of separation of secure embedded systems becomes central: A Trusted Execution Environment is required, in particular for mobile cryptographic applications.

Ideally, this is not connected to the Internet, so it remains original in order to be protected against injections of surveillance code initiated from outside or through the online connection or generally against the upload of data by the operating system and applications.

When the text to be written has been converted to ciphertext, the encrypted capsule should be brought from the TEE platform to an Internet node via a temporary (and ideally based on a protocol change) route, which then forwards the packet accordingly.

Designing a Trusted Execution Environment for any commercial application of the Android or Apple operating system is illusory and contradicts the basic economic idea of many non-open source applications and the operating system.

Entering only ciphertext into a running system or a closed-source application would be complex, but in principle not impossible.

It makes more sense, of course, to use or design open-source software that enables this separation or transfer of ciphertext through various "heartbeats" or relays to prevent the tapping of further user data.

In this sense, the design of the Echo Chip # 1 meets the requirements.

If every started process of an operating system can send home, then encryption should not only be seen as an isolated process, but should also be understood as "Security by Design", even as "Security within a Context".

Even if the Paradigm of Separation and the creation of a Trusted Execution Environment with the Echo Chips remain an initial model, the task of further research is to close the individual risks and/or to analyze encryption processes, how individual applications possibly influence the encryption processes of other applications.

The first and central analysis object here is also the keyboard application, which precedes every plaintext entry and whose potential upload of text copies can only be counteracted by separation.

Remains to be determined, which other applications or functions would be to be separated or to be replaced by open source alternatives.

8.2 Risk Case: Android @ Huawei

The statement that the Android system could be used for Chinese espionage is part of the current trade dispute with the phone company Huawei.

Before US President Trump started the trade war with the Chinese company, Arkansas Senator Tom Cotton expressed his concerns: "Chinese telecom companies like Huawei effectively serve as an intelligence-gathering arm of the Chinese Communist Party, and the administration is right to restrict the use of their products. Chinese components remain a Trojan horse for telecommunications infrastructure around the globe, and the Department of Commerce should deny their adoption entirely" (Cotton 2019).

A trade dispute that led to Huawei wanting to launch its own operating system or at least to use Android without Google support and thus missing all applications from the Google Play Store (Kharpal 2019).

At the same time, it can be seen that there is a cryptographic risk not only in the area of the software (applications depending on the smartphone manufacturer or app store provider as well as the operating system and its user interface), but also in the area of the hardware of the smartphone manufacturer.

Research and Development requirements:

These processes, which have meanwhile accumulated at national level and at the level of hardware manufacturers, are therefore relevant indicators for achieving a sovereign and diverse design that must be supported by nations and manufacturers.

Even if we cannot come up with a national mobile operating system or our own smartphone hardware, at least in cryptography there must be sovereign Trusted Execution Environment platforms in order to be able to implement the cryptographic conversion free of contamination on a mobile basis – if unfamiliar nations and manufacturers should not be able to integrate a "Trojan".

Due to the lack of national mobile operating systems and smartphone hardware manufacturers, the only alternative in the cryptological environment is the design of a separate platform (as it has been projected for Echo Chip #1), which is not inviting to inject a Trojan or to upload data.

Further research will explore the option of creating national or sovereign operating systems and platforms for cryptographic conversion that are separate from regular operations. Separation and export methods are also to be assessed according to their risk potential.

Governments are well advised to invest in national chip production, in hardware companies as well as in their own and open source mobile operating systems for smartphones and to provide appropriate research funds for these. In addition to the aspect of fostering and integrating cryptographic processes in these areas.

8.3 Risk Case: Virus-Scanner Kasperspky et al.

This risk case is about systematic monitoring processes at the entire operating system and application level using Defender and virus scanners. Whether they are called Windows Defender or Kaspersky and Avast or Play Protect: This software can not only send an index of all software processes and hardware used to an American, Russian, Chinese or other central server, but also can scan file content in case of doubt (or without reason) before encryption.

For example, more than 400 million users and 270,000 corporate customers worldwide use technologies from Kaspersky Lab, according to the Russian IT company.

If one wants to have everything protected, one has to show everything and thus to reveal the possibility of copying - and also have the hardware used analyzed.

After Great Britain and the USA instructed all users in the country in September 2017 not to use the Kaspersky software in the future (Nakashima 2017), the Dutch government also joined a year later (Grapperhaus 2018).

The same was true for the Avast virus scanner, which also uploaded and resold user data even from other applications (Cox 2020).

Our current systems for cryptographic conversion are not only well connected online at all times to generate data uploads, but are also well monitored in all processes by the supposed helpers against supposed risks at all times.

How can the control of the actors rule out the same behavior that they want to control or safeguard themselves? As the examples show, certainly not through commitment. Contamination of the meta level, the indexer of the operating system processes and the installed and running applications require more drastic measures than if only a single app uploaded phone books or location data or text entries.

Research and Development requirements:

Programs that index all files, check their contents and formulate protection from them, can not only capture the entire population, but also know exactly which new, unknown and self-compiled files occur.

If all processes are monitored, a self-compiled open source application is immediately noticeable and is reported centrally.

The unknown hash of such an exe or bin would immediately stand out in the negative for self-compiled (encryption) software as well as in the positive for injected malware.

This also speaks in the open source and cryptographic area for an alternative model that operates separately and independently of the indexers.

If the injection options are reduced by separation and upload options are cut off by disconnecting the regular Internet connection, then an indexing protection program might not be necessary?

Because the guardian also has to be updated and can paradoxically be understood as an injection channel.

You may have to conclude that virus monitors are comprehensive monitoring tools, so that there may be greater protection if one does not install them.

One can only trust the indexers to a limited extent, since they rely on the fact that the experience of the individual user from this monitoring process is available to all other users of this software.

The maiden Echo Chip #1 as a Trusted Execution Environment may not need a protective installation at this level.

For the design of an Echo Chip #2 or #3, the congestion control function already provides an analysis of the packets that pass by examining them for duplicates using a hash.

No further malicious (or binary) code (for further execution) can be attached to the encrypted Echo capsule, so the design of the architecture and the surrounding operating system would have to be secured, rather than the processed content, since it is ciphertext.

On Chips #2 and #3, software that monitors and inspects any files or processed packages is basically conceivable, since the encrypted capsules are not broken open by this indexing and remain unaffected.

So far, uploading metadata and telemetry data from routing or forwarding ciphertext has not been the primary goal of defenders and virus scanners, especially since encryption is a further protective layer for this risk case.

For deliberate back doors like a state-run Trojan, one would have to ask whether anti-virus software can also be configured across borders so that such a surveillance Trojan does not work – or whether the user of self-compiled encryption tools is still able to switch off viruses and defender programs integrated in the operating system, to be able to create an open source and self-compiled use of encryption programs "under the radar"[4].

Can users of Veracrypt or GoldBug Crypto Chat Messenger be identified in the central database at the push of a button thanks to Kaspersky, Windows Defender and Co?

If everything is recorded and monitored in the operating system, the self-compiled and open-source encryption programs identified in the central database could be deported instantly and the

---

[4] To describe the self-compiled use of open-source programs as "under the radar" is a logic that can be compared to warnings against encryption because one admits with encryption that one has something to hide. Both linguistic phrases are questionable.

freedom of encryption would be down at its inception.

Does encryption achieve dissident status? In private operation we may not be that far, but in companies the monitoring programs can signal at any time if someone starts an unknown EXE or uses a USB port to inject undefined software (if the USB port is not completely deactivated on the hardware side too).

Further research will therefore show perspectives on how open-source and self-compiled encryption can be integrated through a sovereign freedom in arming up to the deactivation of total security indexers.

In the balance of risk defense with firewall and defender programs, the use of a firewall and the scanning of the entry routes (e.g. e-mail attachments and closing of USB ports) must be strengthened, assuming the total indexing of all files and operating system processes are then more balanced without being able to upload the status reports to central servers.

More firewall instead of virus program and firewall blocks more for outbound traffic instead of inbound traffic.

Further research will also have to investigate the social effects of full indexing of people (compare for China: Schumacher 2019, Sträter 2020) and applications on an equal footing: In the future, will self-compiled open source applications be hunted by total indexers as well as any future defined groups of people, who are totally recorded by facial recognition and other databases? E.g. will smartphones of a full inedexed population regarding a COVID-19 virus medical status information decide if it is allowed to leave the house in case of a pandemic lockdown of the city (comp. Naughton 2020)?

Further research also has to investigate whether encryption helps prevent digital totalitarianism: Do total indexers foster exclusion up to the shutdown of IT system processes, including cryptographic processes, that actually or possibly do not show up conform to the central definition policy?

8.4 Risk Case: BIOS Firmware

The analysis of hardware and its drivers, operational software and its processing of content files as well as the potential upload of these findings - including user, meta and telemetry data - is not only to be analyzed at the operating system level.

Any splash and welcome screen of a BIOS requires microprocessor or controller programming before starting the BIOS, which is already active before the operating system is started.

Who wants to find out whether drivers and other elements can also be reloaded as a result or whether a contact is made to the manufacturer's headquarters and the IP and port are thereby announced?

In numerous forums one can read how to customize the splash screen of a BIOS or how to implement a secure boot.

Christopher Domas, Senior Security Researcher at Intel reports: "Hackers (and researchers) have moved below the OS level and are now targeting firmware – most notably the Unified Extensible Firmware Interface or UEFI (often still referred to as the Basic Input Output System or `BIOS´)" (Domas 2019).

If a BIOS tells the operating system that there is an update for the BIOS, is the BIOS contacting the central web instance or the operating system? BIOS and operating system could just exchange the version to discover updates. So why is not the BIOS extended to update itself over the web? This means this level of chips can also be extended to work like an operating system: to load new code over the net.

However, another case: imagine connections for messaging purposes from MAC to MAC addresses. Why shouldn't a MAC Messenger be designed with e.g. the Address Resolution Protocol (ARP) (RFC 826, Plummer 1982, respective RFC 1122 for IPv6)?

Also, there is for these examples a dilemma in considering encryption: The well-known OSI levels (Zimmermann 1980) are diffused with the plaintext (and probable taped) if the encryption part is done on MAC or Hardware level and not on the level of the Operating System!

Considering this - special injections could be prepared: Probably also a valid context why 5G-Technology from Huawei is considered dangerous, if the drivers of the Hardware are not open source and are capable to auto-load additional updating software that is not audited before the upload.

Research and Development requirements:

Manipulations of firmware - in this case via a software layer that would be incorporated in one of the Echo Chips - would have to be evaluated critically, in particular on Echo Chip #1, such a manipulation could collect information about the entered plaintext.

Even if this information (such as copies of the plaintext and other user data or meta information) could not flow outwards because there is no regular connection to the network for this echo chip, chip designers still remained responsible, to bring safe hardware and safe programming into appropriate Crypto-Chips and secure these (see again Miller et al. 2020).

The outflow of a copy of the entered text would only be conceivable with separation if it took the same route as the export of the Echo-encrypted capsule from Chip #1 to Chip #2.

Ultimately, the user can only be sure that no plaintext entries will flow if his trusted execution environment follows the paradigm of separation or strict isolation from the regular network and the export route is secured.

A transport mechanism may provide data integrity and data privacy. If the source is contaminated, the software is contaminated. Digital signatures, public signatures, digests, etc. provide proofs that certain agents created the products.

They cannot provide proofs that the products are correct regardless of the protocol. TLS is in the regular operation preferred because it provides integrity and privacy: It provides at least data integrity using digests - however, those do not provide data privacy.

A protocol (and also a certain OSI-layer) cannot achieve absolute proof that the product is correct. This can only be provided by separation of the cryptographical conversion process and the export of ciphertext capsules/packets.

There is further research need as to how attackers - across different OSI layers - can influence plaintext encryption processes on other layers.

Security processes must therefore be considered at all levels that get to know the plaintext.

Horizontal contamination prevents an input pad or a Trusted Execution Environment (which as we learned may not be connected to the Internet).

For such a separate conversion tool, protection against vertical contamination (across the OSI layer) must also be taken into account:

Plaintext, which remains deciphered at the operating system level and is only encrypted by hardware, should not run through other layers such as a virtual keyboard (e.g. as with Android), which could monitor itself as an own application or layer in the operating system.

Horizontal and vertical contamination of encryption processes must therefore always be considered in an integrated manner.

An alternative: static firmware, or, interchangeable micro-processors. Imagine: Lego.

8.5 Risk Case: 5G Telecommunication-Chips

Huawei is not only accused of using the Android operating system for tapping user data, but the scope of possibilities also relates to the hardware - also with the 5G telecommunications infrastructure:

Also, the new mobile communication standard 5G attracts the company Huawei again to have little chips in the infrastructure, which are able to update drivers or load additional firmware, which sends information about back-doors to the Chinese company - or even create these back-doors.

The designs of this 5G technology are only known to a few engineers (Pancevski 2020), but it can still be seen that drivers of the hardware can also be updated via a connection to the headquarters (via an API interface, which can be used for lawful listening after a judicial decision). Therefore every update should be subject to a revision. If updated drivers then also allow additional software and other functions to be loaded, it cannot be estimated at present what effects such a design will have in the telecommunications infrastructure in the future and which security gaps could be created. Hence, every un-revisioned update is potentially a Trojan horse!

After the USA, Australia, Japan and Taiwan as well as Canada excluded Huawei network technology for 5G, the exclusion is also being specifically examined in Germany and Europe (Reuters 2019).

Likewise, the listening interests of other countries, such as the USA, or any other national manufacturer, based on hardware drivers, should also be addressed.

The development of security chips therefore not only affects the telecommunications industry, but primarily all #IOT Internet-of-Things devices. Engineers in the IOT industry can learn from the current discussions in the telecommunications industry.

For example, the household appliance manufacturer Miele relies on its own hardware-based protection: „The security chips in the Miele appliances implement end-to-end cryptographic security for larger household appliances such as washing machines, dishwashers or ovens. Since the communication takes place via WLAN and LAN and not via the cellular network, the connectivity of the security chips is guaranteed even if a device - such as a washing machine - is in the basement. The communication is therefore bundled via the routers of the home networks" (Ladner 2020).

Research and Development requirements:

The US government's proposal is therefore to design the software and hardware - in particular the drivers of the hardware - to be open source and launched an open source program for 5G technology with the military research institute DARPA: OPS-5G (DARPA 2020).

The use of open-source fundamentals has long been a well-known postulate in cryptography to enable verifiable aspects of freedom from design errors and back doors - even if their opponents state that bugs cannot be used within proprietary encryption programs because they are less noticeable (e.g. van Valkenburg 2017, comp. to Aumasson 2018).

But who wants to install a proprietary (pre-compiled and not open-source) proxy, for example, if they know that the Chinese also use this application based on the own private IP?

(Since websites in their country are blocked by the Great Firewall, they may have the need to develop a proxy tunnel with a different IP via the development and offer of a closed software proxy application with such a backdoor).

Even those flying a Boeing 747 Max do not want to have undetected bugs in the software that have already caused the plane to crash (comp. Davis 2019).

Bruce Schneier therefore summarizes the need for open-source designs as follows: „Every secret creates a potential failure point. Secrecy, in other words, is a prime cause of brittleness - and therefore something likely to make a system prone to catastrophic collapse. Conversely, openness provides ductility" (Schneier 2002).

How long will it take for security researchers to recognize that numerous products are now being delivered as quasi-satellites with an steady Internet connection to home centers - and that there are numerous security gaps when non-national or non-open source hardware and software or connected devices are used for cryptographic conversion?

Conversely, it also means a need to further develop hardened hardware in the sense of the presented Crypto-Chips in order to keep a balance on this side as well.

Echo chips #1 to #3 must therefore also be designed open source: These and other considerations can be an initiating, presented model, in particular for the further production of hardware and software in the telecommunications industry.

Encryption in conjunction with the hardware and its drivers, as well as BIOS software, especially in telecommunications, can only be created through open-source design and audited certification of source openness.

Open source drivers of telecommunications hardware as well as their certification models have to be established and ways have to be shown, how to foster them through further research.

In addition to BIOS and the drivers, the same applies to integrity protection in the area of memory (comp. suggestions from Chang et al. 2017).

8.6 Risk Case:
Closed Source Operating System Windows

The Windows operating system also uploads data, indexes and user content to Microsoft.

Windows Defender, voice assistant Cortana and other services cannot be switched off completely and other programs such as MS Office store file names and paths as indexes, so that a usage history remains and can be viewed easily if the file or its contents were deleted by the operating system ,

"BackstageInAppNavCache" does not analyze a single file in MS Office, but indexes all files in the path. Means: Opening a Word file on the USB stick indicates all the (and possibly private) files you have brought with you from the UBS stick.

These uploads are then also "encrypted" (Braun 2019, Robrahn et al. 2019, Woll 2019, Krempl 2019).

These processes were uncovered by security researcher Axel Braun and the migration from Linux to Windows in the German financial administration in Lower Saxony was brought before the public prosecutor: AZ NZS 1181 Js 18265/19.

But even the judiciary (let alone politics) wants to approach the case of questioning the security architecture of the popular operating system, which is mono-cultural in business.

In particular, if the world's most widely used operating system sends data home that the user cannot recognize because it is encrypted, such a process should be viewed as critical for any company, particularly in the context of industrial espionage.

Laboratories with secret recipes or operational processes, productions with production data or prices and suppliers for raw materials as well as commercial ideas for innovations are increasingly to be protected by computers that cannot send data out of a company.

Switching to Linux is inevitable, even if it remains utopian due to the applications that require Windows.

Microsoft allows now to dis-able encrypted uploads (builds 14393 and 15063) in the Enterprise and Education versions and is therefore GDPR-compliant for these versions - but not for the Home & Professional versions.

This means, for example, that personal data or e-mails with corresponding attachments from a school may not be processed in the browser or other software of a teacher's private laptop with Windows Professional or Windows Home.

It also means that all professional Windows versions must be updated to the Enterprise (or Education) version, in which the upload of so-called telemetry data can be prevented by an administrator (LDA 2020).

Research and Development requirements:

The paradigm of the separated Trusted Execution Environment of Echo-Chip # 1 can even be regulated for entire operating systems in this analysis:

The computers of a corporate network could remain autonomously separated from the Internet if the employees were not browsing the web and copying content there, or if files had to be sent and received by e-mail.

Research should analyze how these functions work on a second computer, e.g. a surf station that can be outsourced while the work processes take place on another computer that only communicates in the company network.

In this context, the e-mail of the Echo architecture (and clients) allows a relay to be on the Internet and the mailboxes (or reading the Echo mail) to take place on other machines.

With IMAP, the server must be online - and with it the mailbox hosting. With Echo mail this can be separated.

The meaning of a firewall is perverted today: While companies outsource all data and work processes to a cloud and thus make it accessible to third parties, data is simultaneously collected on operating systems that are not open source and sent encrypted from the company to central servers of the operating system manufacturers.

A firewall therefore does not have to ward off external attacks, but firewalls such as Pfsense (Buechler / Pingle 2009) and analysis tools such as WireShark (Nath 2015, Hauser / Huber 2018) need to be further investigated as to, how they can better be able to determine and prevent central servers to transmit encrypted operating data from the operating system from the inside of an organization.

It is therefore important to research methods for stopping data transmission, even if it is in the form of ciphertext, that is not authorized by the user or the company.

8.7 Risk Case:
Closed Internet Networks like #RUNET

Russia reported that it successfully disconnected the domestic Internet, the so-called #RUNET, from the Internet in the rest of the world. This ability would be necessary to protect against a cyber-attack.

Critics emphasize that the population should not be able to communicate freely and read foreign opinions for themselves: It remains critical if history books in education only know one version and interpretation of what is happening (comp. Wakefield 2019, Aguirre 2020).

Here we have an example as a risk case - even recognized by the state - which does not separate a device, not an operating system and not a company network, but also implements the separation of the entire network infrastructure of an entire nation.

Research and Development requirements:

The efforts to decouple the Internet of a certain state government from the general Internet can also be represented by routing (possibly state-certified)

Crypto-Chips and/or cryptographic tokens within programmable Crypto-Chips.

With Adaptive Echo (AE), for example, nodes are excluded from the forwarding if they do not know a specific cryptographic token.

The Inverse Adaptive Echo (IAE) would be the opposite: nodes can only forward a data packet if they know a cryptographic token that matches the packet (comp. Gasakis/Schmidt 2018: 42ff).

At the same time, the routing can also be designed as dedicated servers that are exempt from censorship.

Further research questions arise:
- How can cryptographic token foster and influence routing and beyond routing?
- What do attacks on cryptographic tokens look like and how can they be secured?
- What is the interaction between packet identification and also identification according to a cryptographic token in the respective forwarding machine?
- There is also the research question of how Chinese and Russians can be helped in the face of the respective country firewall, so that websites from abroad can be read with independent reporting?

9 The Secure Architecture Model (SAM) extends and integrates the OSI-Model

In summary, we are already seeing an increase in the grain size of the risk systems: separate chip, separate application, separate operating system, separate company network, separate country network.

The grain sizes of the risk cases just discussed, as well as the knowledge gained when cryptographic processes for secure embedded systems are discussed, then require an expansion of the well-known OSI model - which is based on a Secure Architecture Model (SAM).

The Open Systems Interconnection (OSI) model is a conceptual model that characterizes and standardizes the communication functions of a telecommunication or computing system without regard to its underlying internal structure and technology. The OSI model was first defined in raw form in Washington, DC in February 1978 by Hubert Zimmermann of France and the refined standard was published by the ISO in 1984.

In 1983, these two documents were merged to form a standard called "The Basic Reference Model for Open Systems Interconnection". The standard is usually referred to as Open Systems Interconnection Reference Model, OSI Reference Model, or simply OSI model. It was published in 1984 by both the ISO, as standard ISO 7498, and by the ITU-T (former CCITT) as standard X.200.

The original version of the model had seven layers. A layer serves the layer above it and is served by the layer below it.

01 - Physical layer
02 - Data link layer
03 - Network layer
04 - Transport layer
05 - Session layer
06 - Presentation layer
07 - Application layer

The SAM model starts, where the OSI Model ends: A Secure Architecture Model (SAM) needs to consider the following layers appended to the OSI-Layers. The content of the OSI-Model and bespoken considerations deriving from Cryptography and the thoughts of this essay result in the SAM Model with all 13 layers:

08 - Hardware Supplier Layer
09 - Firmware Programming & Microprocessor Driver Layer
10 - Supplier Layer for Operating System & Software
11 - Operating Processes Guard and Document Indexer Layer
12 - Encryption Layer
13 - (Regional & Global) Stakeholder Strategy & Policy Layer

Figure 2: The Secure Architecture Model (SAM)

Figure 2: Echo on a Chip - The Secure Architecture Model (SAM)

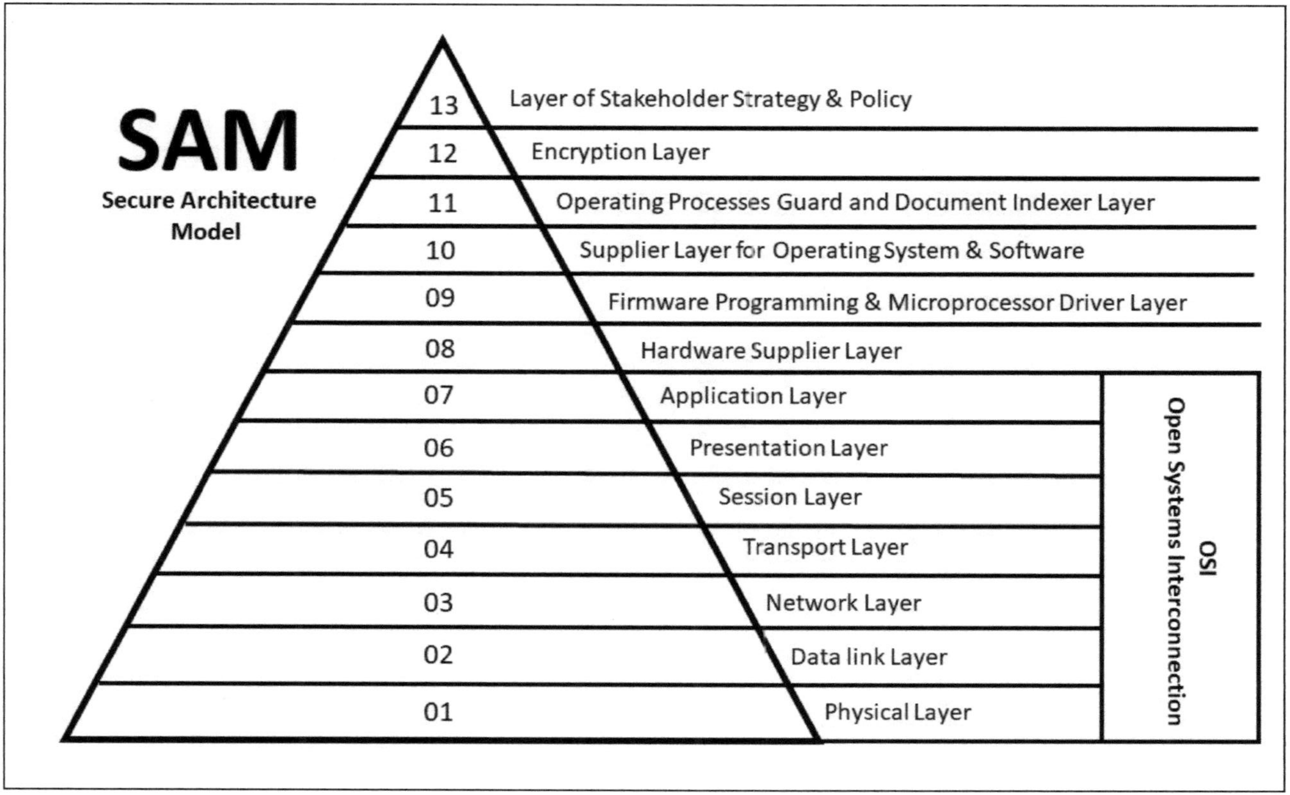

SAM
Secure Architecture Model

13	Layer of Stakeholder Strategy & Policy
12	Encryption Layer
11	Operating Processes Guard and Document Indexer Layer
10	Supplier Layer for Operating System & Software
09	Firmware Programming & Microprocessor Driver Layer
08	Hardware Supplier Layer
07	Application Layer
06	Presentation Layer
05	Session Layer
04	Transport Layer
03	Network Layer
02	Data link Layer
01	Physical Layer

OSI
Open Systems Interconnection

The further layer can be described and justified as follows, starting with the last OSI-Layer: The Application layer:

07: **The Application Layer** considers the Applications and also possibly their Encryption. Application manufacturers consolidate data from users of their applications with all to be reviewed interconnections and risks. This layer is already considered in the OSI-Model.

08: **The Hardware Supplier Layer** considers the suppliers of Hardware, which probably provides additional extensions within Hardware or Software to report to home of the hardware manufacturer. The Hardware supplier layer is more than just the physical layer, as it refers also to the manufacturer and its ethical policy and economic inter-dependencies to others worldwide. The physical layer would not include corruption of a hardware manufacturer in the market behavior; or friendship to certain governments, which includes to sell back-doors to stakeholders, instead of closing gaps. It is in this example closely related to layer 13, see further below.

09: **The Firmware Programming & Microprocessor Driver Layer** simply need to be considered as a dedicated layer to start each Hardware device, e.g. a network card, an USB Stick or in general the BIOS of the machine. This layer is of central importance for the error-free initiation of the machine and justifies its own consideration as an intermediary between hardware and operating system.

10: **The Supplier Layer for Operating System & Software:** This layer must be explicitly added to the OSI model, which stops at the application level, even if one might think that all OSI layers ultimately represent an operating system. However, the sum of the individual parts is not yet a holistic view of an entire operating system. As with the hardware supplier layer, considerations are involved here as to who produces the operating system, which policies exist and how the operation of the system influences encryption processes and data security.

11: **The "Operating Processes Guard and Document Indexer Layer"** is a further dedicated software process. This layer is more than a special application like a Defender or virus guard. We often find this layer integrated into the operating system. It is therefore higher than the operating system, since this layer takes a bird's eye view and indexes and monitors all files and processes.

12: **Encryption Layer:** The encryption layer should also be added as a special focus, since it can or should play a role at all levels when integrated (or not). Instead, this explicit layer combines a central analysis perspective for secure architecture (as e.g. here proposed with EoC #1).

13: **Stakeholder strategy and policy Layer:** With this thirteenth layer, another overarching perspective is integrated into the model, it is about the strategy and policy, which a provider and stakeholder implements (e.g. just company-wide, regional or even global). This can e.g. be the strategy of a country to operate a foreclosed domestic network like #RuNet - like the strategy of a company not to store it in the cloud but on premise - as well as the global recommendation to only send encrypted packets to the Internet.

Scanning tools and functions for the derivation and analysis of plaintext inputs can be placed on each of these described levels, just as separation can take place.

For years, cryptography has primarily dealt with whether encryption itself, the underlying algorithm, is secure.

Whether the ciphertext can be converted back to plaintext. Of course, immediate attacker scenarios were also described, but today they can be found all the more in the context of a comprehensive model.

The fact that Russia, like China, separates from the Internet at the macro level is experiencing a new analytical quality in cryptography, as is the case with the further research needs for the separation of a Trusted Execution Environment for each individual citizen - as described with the Echo Chip #1 model at the micro level.

The expansion of the OSI model to a SA-model, or so-to-say "SAM" model, is necessary because the OSI model originated from an era in which the Internet and encryption was not yet as present as they are today.

There are completely new perspectives when we connect the world via the Internet, encrypt messages on the worldwide journey and operate defacto separation, from the decoupling of a chip, a machine, a company network to the separation of an entire nation from worldwide Internet traffic.

Due to these new perspectives and the risk analyzes of the contamination of the individual levels (as a risk of picking up plaintext or influencing the cryptographic conversion), the application and declination of the SAM model will be more comprehensive farther on.

In particular for the analysis of attack scenarios in the area of encryption and the sending of the encrypted packet, additional layers are emerging, whose potential risks could jeopardize secure encryption and end the way of sending only encrypted packets over the Internet.

Without activating further research needs on the basis of the holistic model presented, the department of cryptography can get into a dead end in its application by any citizen, which also affects the existence of the department.

91

Cryptographic analysis encompasses the entire context of the SAM-model and does not only represent the mathematical calculation of a single algorithm.

To summarize: We are facing the age in which computers, algorithms and databases will not only scan and record the population of humans (including their bio-metric features) "without reason" (Kurz 2020), but also analyze any pronounced sentence that is expressed in text or verbally and transferred over the network.

Is there a totalitarian record of all before with possible filter criteria according to the desired definition? Measures for the filtered target group may not be imagined, especially since they will reach a new dimension with a decentralized execution.

It is a policy referred to SAM-Model Level 13, when EU and some US-States discuss and recommend to forbid face recognition software in public places in general (Fanta 2020, Conger et al. 2019).

Encrypting all packets sent over the Internet can help preserve human freedom. Nevertheless, there are efforts to control the sending of encrypted packets again - at all levels of the SAM model.

Or the future development will give cryptography a general stab in the face. - Not by political decree, but by technical measures.

Kalev Leetaru (2019) points out: "Embedding content scanning tools directly into phones would make it possible to scan all apps [for plaintext], including ones like Crypto Chat Applications, effectively ending the era of encrypted communications. Putting this all together, the sad reality of the encryption debate is that after 30 years it is finally over: dead at the hands of Facebook [and Android and Apple iOS Manufacturer]. While some phone manufacturers could distinguish themselves by offering bespoke phones with custom operating systems that do not include such scanning, such devices are likely to be rare, used only by those who are willing to go to great lengths to escape government scrutiny."

The author's vision of a taping operating system on mobile phones might be already reality on the Application- or Keyboard-Layers or even Operating System layers.

Have American operating systems for smartphones already become a "clipper chip" (comp. Denning 2016), which means that they have already implemented back-doors in the smartphone?

Though: This hard contrast points out at the same time the requirement for a Separated Secure Embedded System (SSES) as Trusted Execution Environment. A separated, unconnected Crypto-Pad to enter and encrypt text and speech is the idea of Echo-Chip #1.

But: The next idea is already proposed: to deactivate unregistered and unconnected operating systems after one day! Then user have no unconnected operating machines, to conduct the cryptographic conversion.

That is today already reality: If one installs Windows 10 with the official installation media from Microsoft, one will be (also in the European or German version) now forced to link the own operating system with an online Microsoft account - if one has an active internet connection. A local account can only be set up if the PC is offline during the installation. What Microsoft originally called a test was then intended to be rolled out across the globe (Geuss 2020).

A perspective: There will be always open source operating systems - thanks to Linux, and Ubuntu Touch operating system for mobile devices.

If other nations, internet nodes or suppliers try to take us by the needle, a technological sovereignty and independence becomes central: as it was evident in the times of the Corona Virus (Covid-19) as well as for the production of medical goods such as masks and test kits against this virus. – For sure, a data and technology sovereignty also applies to processes, algorithms and innovations in the field of cryptography.

The Association of electrical engineering, electronics and information technology (VDE - Verband der Elektrotechnik, Elektronik und Informationstechnik) examined what is necessary to become technically sovereign as a nation: Technological sovereignty is the ability of a state or a society, to be able to implement political and social priorities - without being hampered by insufficient or lack of control over technologies.

It is to be distinguished from self-sufficiency on the one hand and from external determination on the other. For example, Germany and the EU would have to make "massive investments in education and training" with approaches such as "digital classrooms" and programming courses, as well as in research. Above all, the skills in microelectronics and software should be expanded. According to the paper, "open source" communities are helpful.

Especially the information and communication technology is particularly sensitive, since many components have to be sourced internationally. At the same time, the sector is relevant for a large number of industries and represents a critical infrastructure for all of public life. In addition to products such as routers, memory, computers, chips, this also applies to software tools, algorithms and data (VDE 2020).

If separation & isolation is the answer to doubts about trust or the mental assumption of contamination, then trust must experience a sovereignty that puts hardware and software on its own rather than someone else's feet, and thirdly, particularly disconnects Internet connections for cryptographic conversions.

Or Internet traffic is only possible on the basis of encrypted Echo packets of the entry and exit nodes, which allow the transfer to a Trusted Execution Environment:

A "Separate Secure Embedded System" (SSES) like the Echo Chip # 1 represents this in its design par excellence. Designing this separate input and conversion of plaintext is called "going the Extra Mile" (see Nomenclatura op.cit.).

Are we ready to consider going the Extra Mile and will there be further research on hardware, respective Micro-Controllers and Mirco-Porocessors as (Separate) Secure Embedded Systems to support this way?

Cryptography considering the ideas and programming of the Echo and the Extra Mile on Secure Embedded Systems will continue to be an *awake* research area – especially culminating in the design of separated conversion hardware.

10 Literature

Adams, David / Maier, Ann-Kathrin (2016): BIG SEVEN Study, open source crypto-messengers to be compared - or: Comprehensive Confidentiality Review & Audit of GoldBug, Encrypting E-Mail-Client & Secure Instant Messenger, Descriptions, tests and analysis reviews of 20 functions of the application GoldBug based on the essential fields and methods of evaluation of the 8 major international audit manuals for IT security investigations, English / German Language, June 2016, ISBN 9783750408975.

Aguirre, Diego (2020): RuNet: cos'è e come funziona l'internet russo "sovrano", Febbraio 1, URL: https://www.cyberdude.it/2020/02/01/runet-internet-russo-come-funziona/.

Anderson, Ross / Bond, Mike / Clulow, Jolyon / Skorobogatov, Sergei (2005): Cryptographic Processors - A Survey.

Aumasson, Jean-Philippe (2018): Open-Souce Crypto is no better than closed-source Cryoto, URL: https://research.kudelskisecurity.com/2018/10/02/open-source-crypto-is-no-better-than-closed-source-crypto/.

Barr, Michael / Massa, Anthony (2007): Programming Embedded Systems, O'Reilly Sebastopol.

Barthe, L. / Cargnini, L.-V. / Benoit, P / Torres, L. (2011): Optimizing an Open-Source Processor for FPGAs: A Case Study. In Proceedings of the conference on Field Programmable Logic and Application – IEEE, FPL'11, p. 551–556.

Bertram, Linda A. / van Dooble, Gunther (2019): Transformation of Cryptography, ISBN: 9783749450749.

Biedermann, Alexander (Ed.) (2010): Design methodologies for secure embedded systems.

Bitkom (2010): Eingebettete Systeme – Ein strategisches Wachstumsfeld für Deutschland: Anwendungsbeispiele, Zahlen und Trends, URL: https://www.bitkom.org/sites/default/files/pdf/noindex/Publikationen/2010/Leitfaden/Eingebettete-Systeme-Anwendungsbeispiele-Zahlen-und-Trends/EingebetteteSysteme-web.pdf.

Bossuet, L. / Grand, M. / Gaspar, L. / Fischer, V. / Gogniat, G (2013): Architectures of flexible symmetric key cryto engines

— a survey: from hardware coprocessor to multi-crypto-processor system on chip, to be published in the journal ACM Computing Surveys, volume 45, number 4, December, 2013.

Braun, Axel (2019): Windows-Zwangsmigration: Strafanzeige gegen niedersächsische Landesregierung, AZ NZS 1181 Js 18265/19, 2019.

Buechler, Christopher M. / Pingle, Jim (2009): pfSense - the definitive guide to the pfSense open source firewall and router distribution, Reed Media Services.

Catsoulis, John (2005): Designing Embedded Hardware, O'Reilly.

Chang, Rui / et al. (2017): MIPE - a practical memory integrity protection method in a Trusted Execution Environment, in: Cluster Computing (2017) 20: 1075, https://doi.org/10.1007/s10586-017-0833-4.

CHES 19 (2017): Cryptographic hardware and embedded systems - CHES 2017 - 19th International Conference, Taipei, Taiwan.

Cohen, Jon (2020): The power of travel bans - Scientists are racing to model the next moves of a coronavirus that's still hard to predict, February 7, URL: https://www.sciencemag.org/news/2020/02/scientists-are-racing-model-next-moves-coronavirus-thats-still-hard-predict.

Computer History Museum (1960): Metal Oxide Semiconductor (MOS) Transistor Demonstrated - The Silicon Engine: A Timeline of Semiconductors in Computers.

Conger, Kate / Fausset Richard / Kovaleski, Serge F. (2019): San Francisco Bans Facial Recognition Technology, May 14, URL: https://www.nytimes.com/2019/05/14/us/facial-recognition-ban-san-francisco.html.

Cotton, Tom: Chinese components remain a Trojan horse for telecommunications infrastructure around the globe, URL: https://twitter.com/SenTomCotton/status/1128777992195514373 & https://www.cotton.senate.gov/?p=press_release&id=1126.

Cox, Joseph (2020): Leaked Documents Expose the Secretive Market for Your Web Browsing Data - An Avast antivirus subsidiary sells 'Every search. Every click. Every buy. On every site.', January 27, URL: https://www.vice.com/en_us/article/qjdkq7/avast-antivirus-sells-user-browsing-data-investigation.

Cox, Matthew (2019): Army Follows Pentagon Guidance, Bans

Chinese-Owned TikTok App, 30. December 2019, URL: https://www.military.com/daily-news/2019/12/30/army-follows-pentagon-guidance-bans-chinese-owned-tiktok-app.html.

DARPA (2020): Improving 5G Network Security - New program seeks to leverage open source software and systems to address security challenges facing 5G and future wireless networks, URL: https://www.darpa.mil/news-events/2020-02-05.

Davis, Aaron C. / Lazo, Luz / Schemm, Paul (2019): Additional software problem detected in Boeing 737 Max flight control system, officials say, April 2, URL: https://www.washingtonpost.com/world/africa/ethiopia-says-pilots-performed-boeings-recommendations-to-stop-doomed-aircraft-from-diving-urges-review-of-737-max-flight-control-system/2019/04/04/3a125942-4fec-11e9-bdb7-44f948cc0605_story.html.

Denning, Dorothy / Rotenberg, Marc (2016): From Clipper Chip to Smartphones: Unlocking the Encryption Debate, 25. March.

Diffie, Whitfield / Hellman, Martin (1976): New directions in cryptography, 22, IEEE transactions on Information Theory, p. 644-654.

Domas, Christopher: The importance of hardening firmware security at Intel, 17. July 2019, URL: https://www.helpnetsecurity.com/2019/07/17/hardening-firmware-security/.

Edwards, Scott & Spot-On Encryption Suite (2019): Democratization of Multiple & Exponential Encryption: - Handbook and User Manual as practical software guide, ISBN: 9783749435067.

Ernst Michael (2011): Open Source Software und Embedded Systems.

Fairsearch (2013): Beschwerde von 17 Firmen über Smartphone-Betriebssystem Android. Ihr Vorwurf: Google nutze Android als "trojanisches Pferd", April 9, URL: https://www.spiegel.de/netzwelt/web/europaeische-kommission-fairsearch-uebt-kritik-an-google-android-a-893324.html.

Fanta, Alexander (2020): EU erwägt Verbot von Gesichtserkennung, January 17, URL: https://netzpolitik.org/2020/eu-erwaegt-verbot-von-gesichtserkennung/.

Fischer, V. / Drutarovský, M. / Šimka, M. / Celle, F. (2004): Simple

PLL-based True Random Number Generator for Embedded Digital Systems. In Design and Diagnostics of Electronic Circuits and Systems Workshop – DDECS'04, p. 129–136.

Flood, P. / Schukat, M. (2014): Peer to peer authentication for small embedded systems: A zero-knowledge-based approach to security for the Internet of Things, The 10th International Conference on Digital Technologies 2014, Zilina, pp. 68-72.

Flood, Pádraig / Schukat, Michael (2014): Peer to peer authentication for small embedded systems: A zero-knowledge-based approach to security for the Internet of Things, The 10th International Conference on Digital Technologies, Zilina, Slovakia.

Forthmann, Jörg (2016): Google verschluckt sich an seinem Datenhunger, July 12, URL: https://www.welt.de/wirtschaft/bilanz/article161333757/Google -verschluckt-sich-an-seinem-Datenhunger.html.

Fournaris, Apostolos P. / Sklavos, Nicolas (2014): Secure embedded system hardware design – A flexible security and trust enhanced approach, in: Computers & Electrical Engineering, Volume 40, Issue 1, January, Pages 121-133.

Gasakis, Mele / Schmidt, Max: Beyond Cryptographic Routing: The Echo Protocol in the new Era of Exponential Encryption (EEE), 2018, ISBN: 9783748151982.

Gaspar, Lubos (2012): Crypto-processeur – architecture, programmation et évaluation de la sécurité, Group: Secure Embedded Systems, Jean Monnet University.

Geuß, Martin (2020): Windows 10: Zwang zum Microsoft-Konto erreicht Deutschland, 20. Februar, URL: https://www.drwindows.de/news/windows-10-zwang-zum-microsoft-konto-erreicht-deutschland.

Grapperhaus Ferdinand: Voorzorgsmaatregel ten aanzien van gebruik Kaspersky antivirussoftware,15. Mai 2018, URL: https://www.tweedekamer.nl/kamerstukken/brieven_regering/d etail?id=2018Z08634&did=2018D28292.

Guillermin N. (2010): A High Speed Coprocessor for Elliptic Curve Scalar Multiplications over Fp., in: Mangard S. / Standaert FX. (Eds.): Cryptographic Hardware and Embedded Systems, CHES 2010. CHES 2010. Lecture Notes in Computer Science, vol 6225, Springer, Berlin.

Hauser, Bernhard J. / Huber, Bernhard (2018): Netzwerkanalyse mit Wireshark - Einführung in die Protokollanalyse, Haan-Gruiten.

Heiderich, Mario / Horn, Jann / Krein, Nikolai (May 2015): Pentest-Report NitroKey Storage Firmware 05.2015, Cure53.

Hodjat, A. / Verbauwhede, I. (2004): High-throughput programmable cryptocoprocessor. IEEE Micro magazine, 24(3):34–45.

Holland, Martin (2018): Studie: Android übermittelt Standort Hunderte Mal am Tag zu Google, in: Heise online, 22 August.

Hudde, Hans Christoph (2013): Development and Evaluation of a Code-based Cryptography Library for Constrained Devices, Master's Thesis, February 7, URL: https://www.emsec.ruhr-uni-bochum.de/media/attachments/files/2013/03/mastersthesis-hudde-code-based-cryptography-library.pdf.

Kharpal, Arjun (2019): Huawei launches new operating system Harmony OS, URL: https://www.cnbc.com/2019/08/09/huawei-launches-its-own-operating-system-hongmengos-or-harmonyos.html.

Kingsley-Hughes, Adrian (2020): IronKey D300 encrypted USB flash drive gets NATO Restricted Level certification, February 18, URL: https://www.zdnet.com/article/kingston-ironkey-d300-encrypted-usb-flash-drive-gets-nato-restricted-level-certification/.

Kleidermacher, David / Kleidermacher, Mike (2012): Embedded Systems Security - Practical Methods for Safe and Secure Software and Systems Development.

Koç, Çetin K. (2000): Cryptographic hardware and embedded systems - Second international workshop, Worcester, MA, USA, Berlin.

König, Philipp (2013): Deep packet Inspection und das Kommunikationsgeheimnis - die Neutralität des Internets aus dem Blickwinkel der §§ 92 ff TKG, Wien.

Kraan, H.P. (1986): Overzicht Aroflex / Aroflex Overview (Dutch). Internal Memo UNB 20-23- 5180. 7 April.

Krempl, Stefan: Datenschutzkonferenz: Hohe Hürden für den Einsatz von Windows 10 - Die Aufsichtsbehörden haben ein Prüfschema für das Microsoft-Betriebssystem veröffentlicht. Nur bei einem tragbaren Restrisiko kann dieses verwendet werden; 12. November 2019, URL: https://www.heise.de/newsticker/meldung/Datenschutzkonferenz-Hohe-Huerden-fuer-den-Einsatz-von-Windows-10-4584678.html.

Kurz, Constanze (2020): Anlasslose Gesichtserkennung: Das Image der Gesichtserkennung hat dicke Kratzer im Lack - Wir sollten uns gegen Technologien wehren, die uns identifizieren oder aussortieren, 11. Februar, URL: https://causa.tagesspiegel.de/politik/brauchen-wir-die-automatisierte-gesichtserkennung/wir-sollten-uns-gegen-technologien-wehren-die-uns-identifizieren-oder-aussortieren.html.

Ladner, Ralf (2020): Sicherheits-Chips schützen Haushaltsgeräte von Miele, 24. Januar, URL: https://netzpalaver.de/2020/01/24/sicherheits-chips-schuetzen-haushaltsgeraete-von-miele/ & https://www.embedded-computing.com/home-page/security-chips-from-g-d-mobile-security-protect-professional-devices-from-miele#.

Langkamp, Nelson (2007): Secure communication on embedded systems.

LDA Bayern / Bavarian Data Protection Authority for the Private Sector (2020): Windows 10 Investigation Report, URL: https://www.lda.bayern.de/media/windows_10_report.pdf.

Leetaru, Kalev: The Encryption Debate Is Over - Dead At The Hands Of Facebook, 26 July 2019, URL: https://www.forbes.com/sites/kalevleetaru/2019/07/26/the-encryption-debate-is-over-dead-at-the-hands-of-facebook/.

Mazzetti, Mark / Perlroth, Nicole / Bergman, Ronen: It Seemed Like a Popular Chat App. It's Secretly a Spy Tool. ToTok, an Emirati messaging app that has been downloaded to millions of phones, is the latest escalation of a digital arms race, 22. December 2019, URL: https://www.nytimes.com/2019/12/22/us/politics/totok-app-uae.html.

McEliece, Robert J. (1978): A Public-Key Cryptosystem Based On Algebraic Coding Theory, DSN Progress Report. 44: 114–116.

McNoodle Library (2016): Implementation of the McEliece Algorithm in C++, Github.

Mentens, N. (2007): Secure and Efficient Coprocessor Design for Cryptographic Applications on FPGAs. PhD thesis, Ruhr-University Bochum.

Miller, Greg et al. (2020): #Cryptoleaks Rubicon - The intelligence coup of the century - For decades, the CIA read the encrypted communications of allies and adversaries, URL: https://www.washingtonpost.com/graphics/2020/world/national

-security/cia-crypto-encryption-machines-espionage/ & https://www.cryptomuseum.com/intel/cia/rubicon.htm.

Molloy, Derek (2016): Exploring Raspberry Pi - Interfacing to the Real World with Embedded Linux, Wiley.

Mosanya, E. / Teuscher, C. / Restrepo, H. / Galley, P. / Sanchez, E. (1999): Cryptobooster - A reconfigurable and modular cryptographic coprocessor; in: Proceedings of the workshop on Cryptographic Hardware and Embedded Systems – CHES'99, p. 726–726, Springer.

Nakashima, Ellen / Gillum, Jack: National Security: U.S. moves to ban Kaspersky software in federal agencies amid concerns of Russian espionage, 13. September 2017, URL: https://www.washingtonpost.com/world/national-security/us-to-ban-use-of-kaspersky-software-in-federal-agencies-amid-concerns-of-russian-espionage/2017/09/13/36b717d0-989e-11e7-82e4-f1076f6d6152_story.html.

Nath, Anish (2015): Packet analysis with Wireshark - leverage the power of Wireshark to troubleshoot your networking issues by using effective packet analysis techniques and performing an improved protocol analysis, Birmingham.

Naughton, John (2020): Privacy on Parade: For non-intrusive tracking of Covid-19, smartphones have to be smarter, April 11, URL: https://www.theguardian.com/commentisfree/2020/apr/11/for-non-intrusive-tracking-of-covid-19-smartphones-have-to-be-smarter.

Nedospasov, Dmitry; Heiderich, Mario (August 2015): Pentest-Report NitroKey Storage Hardware 08.2015, Cure53.

Newman, Peter (2019): IoT Report: How Internet of Things technology growth is reaching mainstream companies and consumers, January 28, URL: https://www.businessinsider.com/internet-of-things-report?r=DE&IR=T.

Nomenclatura – Encyclopedia of modern Cryptography and Internet Security, ISBN: 9783748191513 & ISBN: 9783746066684.

Pancevski, Bojan (2020): U.S. Officials Say Huawei Can Covertly Access Telecom Networks - Push for allies to block Chinese company, URL: https://www.wsj.com/articles/u-s-officials-say-huawei-can-covertly-access-telecom-networks-11581452256.

Philips Usfa (1982): Internal Memo L/5636/AvdP/JG, 23 August, page 5, cryptomuseum.com.

Plummer, David C. (1982): RFC 826, An Ethernet Address Resolution Protocol -- or -- Converting Network Protocol Addresses to 48.bit Ethernet Address for Transmission on Ethernet Hardware, Internet Engineering Task Force, Network Working Group.

PQCrypto (2019): Post-Quantum Cryptography - 10th International Conference, PQCrypto 2019, Chongqing, China, May 8–10, Cham / Springer.

Preneel, Bart / Bosselaers, Antoon / Govaerts, René / Vandewalle, Joos (1992): A Software Implementation of the McEliece Public-Key Cryptosystem; in: Proceedings of the 13th Symposium on Information Theory in the Benelux, Werkgemeenschap voor Informatie- en Communicatietheorie, pp. 119-126.

Purdum, Jack (2012): Beginning C for Arduino - Learn C Programming for the Arduino and compatible Microcontrollers.

Repka, Marek (2014): McELIECE PKC CALCULATOR, Journal of ELECTRICAL ENGINEERING, VOL. 65, NO. 6, pp. 342–348.

Reuters: Deutsche sehen Zusammenarbeit mit Huawei bei 5G-Netz skeptisch, 18. DEZEMBER 2019, URL: https://de.reuters.com/article/deutschland-huawei-union-idDEKBN1YM11A.

Robrahn, Rasmus / Krämer, Martin Dr. / Lahmann, Christoph Dr. / Robra, Uwe / AK Technik der Konferenz der unabhängigen Datenschutzbehörden des Bundes und der Länder (2019): Datenschutz bei Windows 10 – Prüfschema – Version 1.0, URL: https://tlfdi.de/mam/tlfdi/gesetze/orientierungshilfen/beschluss_zu_top_13_win10_prufschema.pdf.

Roering, Christopher (2013): Coding Theory-Based Cryptopraphy: McEliece Cryptosystems in Sage, Honors Theses. Paper 17, URL: http://digitalcommons.csbsju.edu/honors_theses/17.

Roth, Andreas (2002): Das Microcontroller Kochbuch MCS51, mitp Verlag.

Schmidt, Jürgen / Kolla-ten Venne, Patrick / Eikenberg, Ronald (2012): Selbstbedienungsladen Smartphone - Apps greifen ungeniert persönliche Daten ab. c't, 10. März.

Schneier, Bruce (2002): Homeland Insecurity, URL: https://www.schneier.com/news/archives/2002/09/homeland_insecurity.html.

Schumacher, Samuel (2019): China erzieht das Volk via

Smartphone - Wer auf definierten Seiten surft, hat keinen guten Stand, November 16, URL: https://www.watson.ch/international/digital/399331494-zensur-und-ueberwachung-so-veraendert-china-das-verhalten-seines-volkes.

Shirriff, Ken (2016): The Surprising Story of the First Microprocessors, IEEE Spectrum, Institute of Electrical and Electronics Engineers.

Smoke (2017): Documentation of the Android Messenger Application Smoke with Encryption, URL: https://github.com/textbrowser/smoke/raw/master/Documentation/Smoke.pdf, 2017.

SmokeStack (2017): Server Software for Encrypted Messaging, URL: https://github.com/textbrowser/smokestack .

Soghoian, Chris (2015): URL: Google's lack of support for strong encryption makes second-class citizens out of people who can't afford encrypted devices. URL: https://www.technologyreview.com/s/543161/why-google-trailing-apple-on-encryption-support-is-a-human-rights-issue/.

Spot-On (2011): Documentation of the Spot-On-Application, URL: https://sourceforge.net/p/spot-on/code/HEAD/tree/, under this URL since 06/2013, Sourceforge, including the Spot-On: Documentation of the project draft paper of the pre-research project since 2010, Project Ne.R.D.D., Registered 2010-06-27, URL: https://sourceforge.net/projects/nerdd/ has evolved into Spot-On. Please see http://spot-on.sf.net and URL: https://github.com/textbrowser/spot-on/blob/master/branches/Documentation/RELEASE-NOTES.archived .

Spot-On (2020): Documentation of the Spot-On-Application, URL: https://github.com/textbrowser/spot-on/tree/master/branches/trunk/Documentation, Github 2020.

Stanley, Alyse: TikTok Chalks Up Another Military Ban, 22. December 2019, URL: https://gizmodo.com/tiktok-chalks-up-another-military-ban-1840601422.

Sträter, Andreas: (2020): Überwachung - Wie China seine Bürger mit einem Punktesystem kontrollieren will: China ist auf dem Weg zur totalen Überwachung. Mit einem Punktesystem sollen gute Taten belohnt und schlechte bestraft werden, 30. Januar, URL: https://www.quarks.de/gesellschaft/wie-china-seine-buerger-mit-einem-punktesystem-kontrollieren-will/.

Tomar, Ankur / Kuther, Margit (2020): Die Vorteile des Raspberry Pi 4 für Embedded-Systeme, 30. Januar, URL: https://www.elektronikpraxis.vogel.de/die-vorteile-des-raspberry-pi-4-fuer-embedded-systeme-a-900377/.

Ukil, A / Sen, J. / Koilakonda, S. (2011): Embedded security for Internet of Things, 2011 2nd National Conference on Emerging Trends and Applications in Computer Science, Shillong, pp. 1-6.

Van Valkenburgh, Peter (2017): What is "open source" and why is it important for cryptocurrency and open blockchain projects?, URL: https://coincenter.org/entry/what-is-open-source-and-why-is-it-important-for-cryptocurrency-and-open-blockchain-projects.

VDE (2020): Technologische Souveränität: Vorschlag einer Methodik und Handlungsempfehlungen, Artikelnummer: 10182.

von Matt, Othmar / Schmid, Stefan (2020): Mikro SD Karte Crypto Mobile HC-9100 - Ist das verantwortungslos? Die geheimen Bundesrats-Handys sind mit Hardware von Crypto verschlüsselt, 15. Februar, URL: https://www.tagblatt.ch/schweiz/ist-das-verantwortungslos-die-geheimen-bundesrats-handys-sind-mit-hardware-von-crypto-verschluesselt-ld.1195118.

Wakefield, Jane (2019): Russia 'successfully tests' its unplugged internet, 24. December, BBC, URL, https://www.bbc.com/news/technology-50902496.

Wecker, Dieter (2015): Prozessorentwurf, De Gruyter Oldenbourg-Verlag.

Wiegelmann, Jörg (2011): Softwareentwicklung in C für Mikroprozessoren und Mikrocontroller - C-Programmierung für Embedded-Systeme VDE Verlag.

Wietzke, Joachim (2012): Embedded Technologies - Vom Treiber bis zur Grafik-Anbindung, Berlin/Heidelberg.

Woll, John: Aufsichtsbehörde: Windows 10 funkt ständig, Einsatz kaum möglich, 12. November 2019, URL: https://winfuture.de/news,112354.html.

Wollinger, Thomas / Guajardo, Jorge / Paar, Christof (2003): Cryptography in Embedded Systems: An Overview - Proceedings of the Embedded World 2003 Exhibition and Conference, pp. 735-744.

Wüst, Klaus (2008): Mikroprozessortechnik - Grundlagen, Architekturen und Programmierung von Mikroprozessoren, Mikrocontrollern und Signalprozessoren, Vieweg und Teubner.

Yan-ling, X. / Wei, P. / Xin-guo, Z. (2008): Design and Implementation of Secure Embedded Systems Based on Trustzone, 2008 International Conference on Embedded Software and Systems, Sichuan, pp. 136-141.

Zimmermann, Hubert (1980): OSI Reference Model — The ISO Model of Architecture for Open Systems Interconnection". IEEE Transactions on Communications. 28 (4): 425–432.

Zimmermann, Karl-Heinz (2019): Curves, cryptography and quantum computing, Uni Hamburg (Embedded Systems).

ZVEI / Zentralverband Elektrotechnik und Elektronikindustrie (2016): Nationale Roadmap Embedded Systems, URL: http://netzwerk-zukunft-industrie.de/wp-content/uploads/2016/01/Anlage-3_Nationale-Roadmap-Embedded-Systems.pdf

11 Didactical Questions

a) Describe the historical development of microprocessor-based machines for encryption.

b) Which components describe the Transformation of Cryptography?

c) Which encryption programs exist for single board computers like Raspberry Pi, Arduino and others?

d) Evaluate and present a self-compiled encryption program for the Raspberry Pi.

e) What is the Echo protocol and what are its basic properties?

f) Form three groups, each presenting and discussing the functions of an Echo Chip.

g) Echo Chip #1 follows the separation paradigm: what does it mean?

h) Present the concept of a Trusted Execution Environment in a conceptual comparison of different authors.

i) Create and develop a program code based on the existing program code of the Echo applications in Java or C++ for one of the three designs of an Echo Chip.

j) Present a risk case and discuss why it is still relevant today.

k) Research from a technical perspective why and how 5G technology should and can be vulnerable to espionage.

l) Discuss the social opportunities and risks involved in separating a device for encryption for the individual as well as in separating the Internet of an entire nation from the wider Internet.

m) Introduce and describe the Secure Architecture (SAM) model and how it integrates the OSI model.

n) Discuss the layers added in the SAM model using referenced, current examples.

o) Check arguments for and against an indiscriminate registration of people and describe which technologies could be used and which should not be used. Justify this in each case and find representatives of the respective arguments.

p) Introduce others in regard of the potentials and risks of the facial recognition technology and describe possible social consequences, if a face - in spite of a text - cannot be disguised - like plaintext is converted to ciphertext.

Based on the historical development of so-called Crypto Chips, the current Transformation of Cryptography shows numerous changes, innovations and new process designs in the field of Cryptography, which also need to be integrated in a hardware design of Microprocessors and Microcontrollers for a Secure Embedded System.

Using the example of the encrypting Echo protocol, a design of a hardware architecture based on three Chips is presented: The central Echo Chip #1 represents a "Trusted Execution Environment" (TEE), which is not connected to the Internet for the conversion processes from plain text to cipher text and is supposed to remain quasi original, to prevent software injections or possible uploads of copies of the plain text. The technical specifications of all three Microprocessors are described in detail.

The established paradigm of separation is recognized as a security feature and discussed as a perception for a Next Generation of Microcontrollers in the field of Mobile Messaging under the technical term "Going the Extra Mile".

This security architecture is then discussed in the context of seven different current risk cases with the consolidated result that the well-known OSI (Open Systems Interconnection) Model is expanded to the Secure Architecture Model, abbreviated SAM.

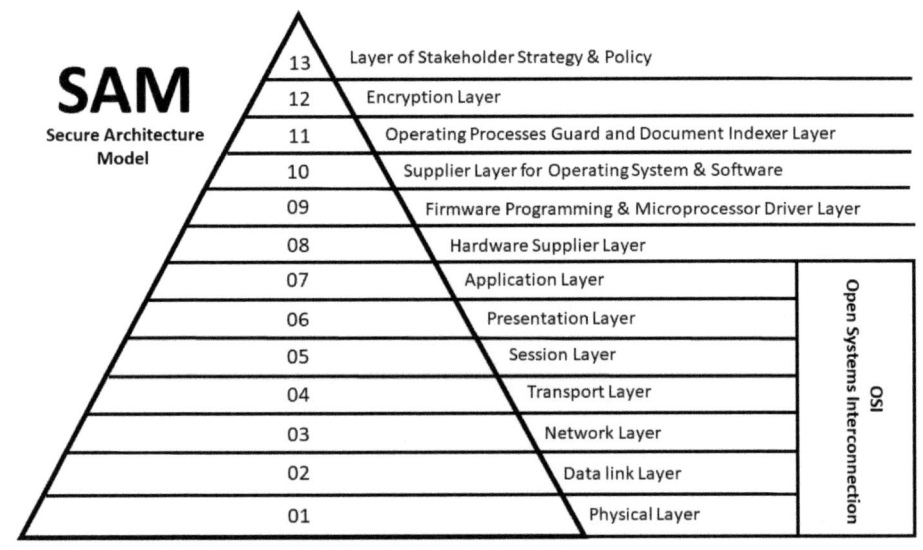

SAM
Secure Architecture Model

13	Layer of Stakeholder Strategy & Policy
12	Encryption Layer
11	Operating Processes Guard and Document Indexer Layer
10	Supplier Layer for Operating System & Software
09	Firmware Programming & Microprocessor Driver Layer
08	Hardware Supplier Layer
07	Application Layer
06	Presentation Layer
05	Session Layer
04	Transport Layer
03	Network Layer
02	Data link Layer
01	Physical Layer

OSI — Open Systems Interconnection

9 783751 916448